CONVERSATIONS ON CREATIVE PROCESS, METHODS, RESEARCH AND PRACTICE

Conversations on Creative Process, Methods, Research and Practice provides unique insights into the experiences of eight established creative practitioners who use their creative process in a professional and personal context. Each of them details their creative processes and how being creative has helped them to achieve a fulfilling work/life balance.

Interviewees discuss how their creativity has helped them to overcome challenges or difficulties they have faced in their lives including grief, health issues, prejudice, divorce, maternity and creative blocks. This book uses original material – research and interviews – to explore the nature of the creative process from the perspective of understanding the activities, thoughts and feelings that shape an individual artist's creative practice and how this might inform a wider collective understanding of creativity and how it can help us to live well. The book suggests that individual creative practice is a means of coming to know the self and your place in the world a little better and perhaps a little differently.

This innovative book is suitable for students, scholars and practitioners using creative and arts-based research and methods in a wide range of disciplines and subjects including the social sciences, education, creative writing and communication and media studies.

Christina Reading is an independent artist and writer who lives and works in Brighton. She studied at Central St Martins School of Institute of Art & Design, London, The University of the Creative Arts, Farnham, and The University of Brighton, UK.

Jess Moriarty is a Principal Lecturer in Creative Writing at the University of Brighton, UK, where she leads the Creative Writing MA and is Co-director of the Centre for Arts and Wellbeing. Jess is a Senior Fellow of the Higher Education Academy and has published extensively on autoethnography and creative writing pedagogy.

CONVERSATIONS ON CREATIVE PROCESS, METHODS, RESEARCH AND PRACTICE

Feminist Approaches to Nurturing the Creative Self

Edited by Christina Reading and Jess Moriarty

Routledge
Taylor & Francis Group

LONDON AND NEW YORK

Designed cover image: Walking and talking (2023). Christina Reading

First published 2024
by Routledge
4 Park Square, Milton Park, Abingdon, Oxon OX14 4RN

and by Routledge
605 Third Avenue, New York, NY 10158

Routledge is an imprint of the Taylor & Francis Group, an informa business

British Library Cataloguing-in-Publication Data
A catalogue record for this book is available from the British Library

ISBN: 978-1-032-25998-7 (hbk)
ISBN: 978-1-032-25999-4 (pbk)
ISBN: 978-1-003-28604-2 (ebk)

DOI: 10.4324/9781003286042

Typeset in Optima
by SPi Technologies India Pvt Ltd (Straive)

We want to thank and cheer for the incredible women who took part in this book and inspired us with their creativity, wisdom, expertise and passion.

This book is for our inner critics – to keep you quiet, for now.

This book is for our families, with our love.

CONTENTS

CREATIVE CONVERSATIONS

Introduction

Jess Moriarty

We both got cancer within a year of each other – fuck you, cancer – and for the same and also for different reasons, it left us both feeling lost. Lost because we did not know who these sick women with cancer were and lost because we didn't want to know them. Lost creatively because we felt our creative practice had been stifled – Chris because the paints she used in her artwork are known carcinogens, and me because of my acute realisation that I was addicted to work: to the admin, meetings and committees that all took me away from writing and teaching and left me feeling empty and purposeless. And lost because we didn't know the way back.

Illness brought change, a change that impacted on our understanding of ourselves and our perspective on the world. We both felt our creativity had withered, that illness had hampered us and our practices of art and writing. But in our last book, *Walking for Creative Recovery* (Reading & Moriarty, 2022), we developed a way of being in our research and art-practice (text and image) that revitalized our creativity in a way that was exciting, surprising and profound. We believe that the method of walking/doing, discussion/reflecting and making can and will inspire, re-engage and potentially reshape notions of individual creativity. This practice, unsure and tentative at first, moved us through our experiences with cancer and creative blocks, helping us to pro-duce new work. Drawing on our personal histories and autobiographical experiences and exploring these directly and indirectly in our practice brought us from the hibernation of cancer and the effects of the global pandemic into a creatively rich and fertile time.

In this book, we are looking to extend this spring-like state by getting out of our own heads – useful and needed during cancer and perhaps inevitable during the pandemic – and connect with other creative people to discover

DOI: 10.4324/9781003286042-1

their experiences of creativity and how they have come to know, appreciate and use their creative wisdom to develop their careers and to see if, like us, this process also offers tools they can apply to their personal lives and living well. Speaking to seven creative professionals at the height of their respective creative careers and using those conversations to frame and direct chapters that explore creativity has generated ideas and tasks that we hope will support readers of this book to enliven and evolve their own creative endeavours, reflect on what their creativity might now need and plan to further legitimise and sustain their creative lives.

Chris and I identify as arts-based researchers, and our way of working combines the crafts of writing and art to tell stories. Scott-Hoy and Ellis argue that "[t]he art part of the project, which creates moods and images, combines with writing, which is better at directing emotion. In many cases, published words are used more to explain the art, rather than enhance the emotional mood".

In this book, we choose not to make the distinction; instead, image, interview and text work together to develop a transdisciplinary text that weaves our creative research, autobiographical experiences with creativity and the transcripts of our conversations together in a single narrative. To educational researchers, such as Tierney and Lincoln (1997), memoir, poetry, painting offer an insight into a multi-layered and complex time (feeling creatively stifled post-cancer) and the process (walking and making) used to move past it. This book contributes to arts-based inquiry experiments seeking to offer alternative ways to transform what is in our consciousness into a public form that others can engage with (Eisner, 1997). Other arts-based researchers are also examining the intersections of talking, walking, art, education, qualitative and/or autoethnographic research (e.g., Clark-Keefe, 2002; Mullen, 2003; Saarnivaara, 2000, 2003; Saarnivaara and Bochner, 2003), and we – Chris and I – argue that this approach offers a multi-layered and evocative text that is personal, academic, creative – which reflects how we live our lives.

The book offers a "meeting place as a mixed stream of fluids, as something multi-layered, not known, always to be created anew, as the field of many understandings" (Sava and Nuutinen, 2003, p. 532) that is connected to notions of intertextuality and the dialogue of texts (Bakhtin, 1981). At the centre of this mixed stream are our conversations with Griz, Thomasina, Lisa, Anna, Irene, Katarina and Sonia. Margaret Wheatley identifies conversations as being the simplest way to restore hope, suggesting that by sharing our stories, problems will lessen and we will feel more able to cope with an uncertain future (Wheatley, 2002) and for us, speaking to other creative professionals has invigorated our own sense of our creative practice and how we might inspire it with what we learned from these amazing women. Covid created an unknown time, and as we all emerge from the enforced fallow time that the pandemic brought, political, environmental and personal landscapes are altered. There is a new terrain that needs to be navigated, mapped and traversed, and this book suggests ideas and tasks to support individual creativity to find a way through this time. Paulo Freire suggests that in order to escape or change bleak situations, humanity requires a politics of hope and the ability to love and trust fellow humans, no matter how broken the world seems. It stems from "an ontological need" (Freire, 1994, p. 10) and we have learnt that dialogue and creativity can not only ease us back into life post-Covid and past cancer; it also offers us a way to process and reconnect after what has come to pass. Co-production has always had an important role to play in rethinking and remaking the world for the better (Daykin et al., 2017), and our way of working relies on collaboration, on valuing others and on hope.

The book is focused around three key concepts:

1 Identifying your individual creative needs and ambitions – where is your creativity at? What does your creativity need? And tasks for addressing these issues.
2 Learning from other practitioners/professionals/makers and how they have navigated and led their own creative recovery.
3 Sharing our responses to the conversation and our own experiences of creativity.

Each chapter has been organised around a particular structure: research, a conversation and a piece of writing where we suggest a task to help the reader support their own creative development. Developing the book in this way was a deliberate attempt to extend the feeling of connection and creative support that the conversations gave us, widening this community to include you, the reader.

Conversations with Other Creative Practitioners

One strand of the book is a series of conversations with seven women artists about their own creative recoveries. These women were selected because of their diverse and innovative creative practices, but we accept that it is not fully inclusive and that inevitably, we have not – and would not – claim that this book is representative of women in the creative industries; not even close. We are conscious of who has been left out and how that might direct our future work, to draw in people from marginalized and underrepresented communities and groups to centre their experiences. The women we were lucky enough to work with were:

• Professor Ann Abraham. E. Paul Torrance Professor for Creativity and Gifted Education and Director of the Torrance Center for Creativity and Talent Development at the College of Education at the University of Georgia (UGA) in Athens, USA.

- Irene Marot, actress and artist.
- Grizelda, cartoonist.
- Katarina Ranković, PhD student in Fine Art at the Goldsmith University.
- Sonia Overall, writer and academic at the University of Canterbury.
- Lisa Norman, events organiser (The Great Escape, Wilderness and Brighton Pride)
- Thomasina Gibson, filmmaker and writer.

These conversations were conducted by Zoom. This had the advantage of allowing the interviewee to talk from the comfort of their own home, but it did mean that we did not meet the women in person, and there is perhaps some regret for us in that because these were women who we admired and looked up to as creative practitioners and were eager to learn from them. On the other hand, Zoom made it easier for us to record the interview and this was sometimes helpful when we were writing up the findings. The exception was the conversation with Irene Marot, which was conducted at her home face to face. We are enormously grateful for the time that the interviewees gave us and for their generous and insightful words. All of our interviewees signed consent forms and were invited to read the transcripts and edit them before publication. We felt this was an important way of developing trust and mutual respect and to ensure the women we interviewed felt our process was ethical and inclusive. We also applied to the University of Brighton's ethics committee to ensure that our interview process was scrutinized by an expert panel.

The questions we discussed included but were not restricted to:

1 What is your earliest memory of being creative?
2 How did you encourage your creativity or what/who inspired it?
3 Do you have an inner critic and how do you work with/against that?
4 When and where are you most creative? What are the tools/space/people you need?
5 How does it feel when it all comes together and works? Do you have an example?
6 What are the things that hinder or demotivate your creativity?
7 Can you think of a specific time or event when you hit a wall? (This could be anything – Covid-19, doing a job that was not right, health, a time when it just seemed frozen. Completely up to you what you choose to share and how personal/practical/professional it is.)
8 How did you get through/round/past?
9 What is the best advice you've had?
10 What does your creativity need?
11 Where do you hope you go next with your creativity?

Creative Tasks for the Reader

In this final strand, we set tasks for the reader at the end of each chapter, extending the *Creative Conversation* to you and opening up space for you to reflect on, and also nurture, your own creative processes. The emphasis here is on motivating and moving our creativity, to value new and old ways of being creative and see them as an essential part of our lives and who we are.

Working in this way, we have created an accessible model with a series of creative tasks to support and encourage your creativity and help you come to know and celebrate your creative self.

Creative Task: Set Intentions and Share Your Aspirations for Your Creativity

Set your intention – what do you want to get out of reading this book? Use a notepad, journal or computer to reflect on the following questions:

- What does your creativity need right now?
- What do you discover about yourself and your process?
- What now?

Use the reflection on your experience of this mini-project to set an intention for your creative practice going forward. What now? Keep moving.

Bibliography

Bakhtin, M. M. (1981). *The dialogic imagination*. For essays by M. M. Bakhtin (C. Emerson & M. Holquist, Trans, M. Holquist, Ed.). University of Texas Press.

Barone, T. (2003). Challenging the educational imaginary: Issues of form, substance, and quality in film-based research. *Qualitative Inquiry, 9*, 202–207.

Clark-Keefe, K. (2002). A fine line: Integrating art and fieldwork in the study of self-conceptualization and educational experiences [CD-ROM]. *Alberta Journal of Educational Research, XLVIII*(3), 1–27.

Daykin, N., Gray, K., McCree, M., & Willis, J., (2017). Creative and credible evaluation for arts, health and well-being: opportunities and challenges of co-production. *Arts & Health, 9*(2), 123–138. DOI: 10.1080/17533015.2016.1206948

Eisner, E. (1997). *The educational imagination: On the design and evaluation of school programs* (3rd ed.). Macmillan.

Freire, P. (1994). *Pedagogy of hope*. Continuum.

Mullen, C. A. (2003). Guest Editor's Introduction: "A Self-Fashioned Gallery of Aesthetic Practice". *Qualitative Inquiry, 9*(2), 165–181. https://doi.org/10.1177/1077800402250927

Reading, C., & Moriarty, J. (2022). *Walking for creative recovery: A handbook for creatives with insights and ideas for supporting your creative life*. Triarchy Press.

Saarnivaara, M. (2000). The boundary within me: Reflections on the difficulty of transgression. *Auto/Biography, 8*(1&2), 56–61.

Saarnivaara, M. (2003). Art as inquiry: The autopsy of an [art] experience. *Qualitative Inquiry*, 9, 580–602.

Saarnivaara, M., & Bochner, A. (2003). At the meeting place of word and picture. *Qualitative Inquiry*, 9(4), 515–534.

Sava, I., & Nuutinen, K. (2003). At the meeting place of word and picture: Between art and inquiry. *Qualitative Inquiry*, 9(4), 515–534. DOI: 10.1177/1077800403254218

Scott-Hoy, K., & Ellis, C. (2008). Wording Pictures: Discovering Heartful Autoethnography in Handbook of the Arts in *Qualitative Research: Perspectives, Methodologies, Examples, and Issues*. SAGE. ISBN: 9781412905312, Online ISBN: 9781452226545. DOI: http://dx.doi.org/10.4135/9781452226545.n11 (pp. 127–141).

Slattery, P. (2001). The educational researcher as artist working within. *Qualitative Inquiry*, 7(3), 370–398.

Tierney, W., & Lincoln, Y. (Eds.) (1997). *Representation and the text: Re-framing the narrative voice*. State University of New York Press.

Wheatley, M. (2002). Turning to one another: Simple conversations to restore hope to the future. *The Journal for Quality and Participation*, 25(2), 8.

1

THE SCIENCE OF CREATIVITY

A Conversation with Anna Abraham

Christina Reading

FIGURE 1.1 Anna Abraham © Ricky Adam.

DOI: 10.4324/9781003286042-2

Anna's research explores the psychological and neural underpinnings of creativity and other aspects of the human imagination, including the reality/fiction distinction, mental time travel, self-referential thinking and mental state reasoning. Her educational and professional training has been within the disciplines of psychology and neuroscience in several academic institutions across the world. She is the author of numerous publications, including *The Neuroscience of Creativity* (2018) and *The Cambridge Handbook of the Imagination* (2020).

Anna was meant to have taken up her new post as Professor for Creativity and Gifted Education and Director of the Torrance Center for Creativity and Talent Development at the College of Education at the University of Georgia (UGA) in Athens, USA, but lockdown in the UK and the imposition of worldwide travel restrictions has meant that at the time of our conversation, she is still waiting for the US travel ban to lift – waiting it out in her half-empty home in York, between continents, between countries, juggling work and single parenthood. Amongst all the challenges presented by these uncertainties, I felt very lucky that she made time to talk to me.

Christina: *Perhaps you could begin by telling me about your interest in creativity and what you are doing now.*

Anna: It's a strange situation at the moment because I'm officially not working in the UK but I am stuck here; the travel ban was imposed a week before I was due to fly out to America to take up my new post, so it feels odd to say I am working at the University of Georgia. It is such an exciting opportunity for me, and I am waiting for the ban to lift so I can start working properly, as opposed to meeting everybody over Skype. With the Covid-19 public health crisis and the Black Lives Matter movement taking centre-stage globally – and everybody being affected by it, students and staff from what I can see – I think UGA is dealing with it all very well by actively engaging with the concerns in an open and supportive manner. I'm very happy to go where I am going because it's so encouraging to see the way both academic faculty and administrative staff are pulling together. They have managed to avoid knee-jerk, unwise reactions, by dealing with the situation head-on and with empathy. On the one hand, this inability to travel has been kind of advantageous for me. I'm a little relieved to not be in the position of starting a new job in a new unfamiliar country in person with my son, who has special needs, in the thick of such challenging times. It's so heartening though to get a sense of what's been done there, be a part of the conversation, get a clear sense how it's going to impact us, and to see how important and lucky we are to have good leadership in such tumultuous times.

Christina: *What role will you be taking up there?*

Anna: My boss has said that I will have three hats on, so to speak. I am
             the E. Paul Torrance Professor for Creativity and Gifted Education
             in the Department of Educational Psychology – so that's one role.
             The Department of Educational Psychology in the College of
             Education has a couple of unique focuses, and one is in the field
             of Gifted Education and Creativity, so I will be part of that teach-
             ing unit there. My second role is to be the new Director of the
             Torrance Centre for Creativity and Talent Development, which is
             really exciting because the focus is on creativity, not just in rela-
             tion to research, but also in relation to community outreach and
             service. I am looking forward to steering the Centre to actively
             drive community-based action. It already carries out wonderful
             training programs for children. Teacher training is also a big focus
             in terms of recognising and nurturing creativity in the classroom.
             We are going to expand the focus further by targeting the wider
             community, older and younger. And finally, my third hat is my
             role as a researcher, where I will continue to study creativity and
             the imagination from a psychological and neuroscientific per-
             spective. So those are my three hats.

Christina: *My understanding is that your background is in neuroscience and
             the boundary between neuroscience and psychology? Is that
             right?*

Anna: My background is in Psychology and Neuroscience. My degree in
             India was in Psychology and then I did an MSc in Psychology in
             the UK and then I went on to do a PhD in Neuroscience in
             Germany.

Christina: *I wanted to approach the interview in two ways: I am interested
             in your own creativity and your own experiences because you
             must be a very creative person to navigate your way through what
             you have done so far, to find your own path through academic
             life, but also in your perspective on those questions as an aca-
             demic and researcher.*

             *So, if I start off by asking about early memories of being crea-
             tive. How important do you think they are to you and how impor-
             tant generally do you think they are? That early experience of
             being creative?*

Anna: My early memories of being creative are incredibly important to
             me. But one is not always aware that one is being creative in the
             moment; I certainly wasn't at that age and it was only when
             I looked at your questions, I thought *hmmmm, what is my earliest
             memory of being creative?* My earliest conscious memory of
             being in the presence of creativity comes from my brother.

I remember recognising him as a creative being. And it was in the most classic way that we recognise creativity in that he had great visual artistic talent. He was great at sketching, and I would just look on in amazement. He even had beautiful handwriting. And I would think, where is this coming from? He's such an idiot [laughter], playing the fool all the time, and yet he creates all this beauty. Not that he's an idiot, you know. It's just the way we talk with one another. Constant light teasing. He was naughty and mischievous and lazy. Yet just somehow, he still had the discipline and skills to sit for hours and sketch. So, I think when I was much younger, in the first five or six years of my life, I recognised it first in him. The act of creativity.

And I think we split our creative talents without realising it. I could see that his abilities were appreciated and it was unusual – given our decidedly non-artistic family background and community – for artistic abilities to be encouraged or appreciated, especially amongst boys. I think my brother and I had a healthy competitive streak between us. We both played musical instruments. That domain belonged to both of us: he was the visual artist with the sketching and the painting, whereas I felt as if my creative side came out on the stage when I was young. My early memories are tied to the theatre. It is such an interesting question though. What is my earliest memory? I do remember telling a lot of tall tales to get out of trouble if that counts as creativity [laughter]. I remember making up lyrics to songs and I love to sing, and I love to imitate characters and make up stuff. As little kids, we always had family and friends over, and the kids were left to their own devices. And a cousin of mine and me would always crawl under the table where the grownups were sitting and pretend their legs were talking.

Christina: *Your performances sound quite community and family based?*

Anna: Not publicly. There was a sort of theatricality to make that that kind of performance, but it was quite private. Between me and one other person at the most.

Christina: *Did you pursue that theatricality? You weren't tempted to go down that road?*

Anna: I did. That is the great thing about going to school, right? If you are lucky enough to go to the kind of school that has good arts and theatre programmes, or at least something where people can mess about and have fun, then you can pursue those fancies. And I did a lot of that. That was the kind of stuff I cared about most as a kid. I was not interested in academia *at all* [laughter]. It was so boring to me compared to the ability to sing in a choir or do sports or act in school plays or even direct them. So, I was not at all interested in academia through most of my education. I came to it extremely late.

There was a lot of negativity associated with being an artist. Also, I just could not find any formal avenues for such interests to be pursued at the time; it was quite a blow to me when I was growing up that I could not do it because there was no opportunity to do so.

Christina: *And do you remember that process of having to let go of that interest and shift your perspective?*

Anna: Yes, it was over one day. That was it. The end of school marked the end of many things, including the ability to pursue theatre. You know, it's one thing I try to emphasise in conversation on education and creativity, we focus so much on creativity in school educational curriculums and how to nurture it and what's necessary, but there is little focus on what happens once you leave school; that's where the support net falls. Because if you were going to continue to pursue your interests as an adult, then you must have accessible, inclusive avenues where you explore this in ways that are quite amateurish. You don't have to be the best at something to want to create. You are probably going to go to an art school if you're clearly the best or very talented. Whereas the nice thing about having more accessible programmes in the community is that you can just dabble to the extent that you want to and discover for yourself what kind of abilities you are capable of developing. But such avenues don't exist a lot of the time. So, I think that's where the net falls. You become an adult and suddenly you are in another realm. No more child time. No more play.

Christina: *What age was that? When the net fell?*

Anna: I was 17 when I finished school, going on 18, basically. I went to college and there was a theatre programme, but I went to college in the north of India and I didn't speak the local language very well. The college did have a great theatre programme, but it was mostly in Hindi. And my language ability was not up to speed to be even part of the community, much less the drama club. I remember feeling a complete blow then, and a really good friend of mine was in Madras, in the south of India, and her college had drama clubs in multiple languages, and she was telling me about all this stuff that she was doing, and I remember thinking, I should have gone there instead; if I could just do it (theatre) on the side it would make life worthwhile. I tried to pursue theatre outside of university but I think I saw the professional side too soon. Or maybe I was too naïve. Either way, it was corrupt and soulless and awful. And I decided that it was not for me because the part of the industry that I saw wasn't about the Arts really. It was more about egos and money.

Christina: *That sounds quite difficult. One of the things I picked up from the paper that you wrote on creativity whilst at Leeds (Abraham, 2015) was women finding it challenging converting that early interest in creativity into a professional avenue. And that there are differences in the way that men seem to be able to do that. Would you like to say a little more about that in terms of the work that you have done?*

Anna: Specific cultural differences obviously make a huge difference here too but there are clear gender differences universally in terms of opportunities and expectations that are given and afforded to girls and boys and men and women. We occupy different spaces in many ways. Having said that, a lot is changing now, and I think the pressure on girls is ever-changing. First, girls needed to be educated. Let us give them a place in the classroom. Then girls need to stop being pushed into these gender-delimited interest spaces and subject spaces. Let us make all spaces open for everyone. I think we have reached that stage now where lots of girls clearly show a lot of interest and promise in STEM (Science, Technology, Engineering and Maths) studies and so on. So, there is a lot of progress in that regard. The counterpoint is understanding what is happening with boys. Fewer boys are going to university, and there is increasingly more learning disability in early childhood amongst boys. Something has gone amiss there, and we need to be able to cater to the needs and strengths of all children, girls and boys alike.

In terms of the Arts, I think girls and boys are equally affected. I don't think either boys or girls are really encouraged to go into the Arts, but if one side is being discouraged more, this reflects chiefly cultural practices. In some cultures, the Arts are seen as a more female discipline and girls are quite happily encouraged to go down that path, but they are now also encouraged to go down the Science route. Boys tend to still be discouraged from going down the artistic route. Nonetheless, if they do it, they do still have more support out there down the line.

The studies that have looked at creative productivity and the factors that affect it indicate that women are making a lot of decisions in their early 20s, not only about where to study and what to do, but also if and when they want families. There are all these conflicting expectations on them. Whereas men don't have the same pressure, not to the same extent. Men can decide to have a child at 20 or 30 or 40 or even later, so the pressures on women are just so different. Part of it is societal, part of it is the way our biology works, which plays a role in when certain instincts kick in. And part of it too is that there is no support structure in place for women who decide to have a family. We decide to have children and we decide to come back to work as well. So, it's a very mixed and complex picture. But I wouldn't make the blanket statement that only girls are disadvantaged. But I do think the elements of pressure that are creeping in for women are just more onerous. Because on one hand, you have people's expectations – *You've been given this big boost! Oh go be an engineer!* – but also, be all the other things. So, they are getting a lot of encouragement but with that they are getting a lot of pressure to reach ever greater heights. On the male side, practices and structures are often instituted in their favour, but I don't think people are looking out for the men and the boys. There is a neglect happening there too. Combine that with this emphatic pressure on the other side and the fact that we all must grapple with so much together; I think it's hard.

Christina: *I was also interested in the fact that in your new role you are going to be extending creativity into the community, and I wonder if that's about trying to ensure that there is a scaffold, a bridge for creativity from education into community and into the professional life. Is there something in that?*

Anna: I feel very strongly that adults are being let down, and this is not only from my own personal experience. We have this seismic shift from the time you turn 18; as adults we must make decisions for ourselves. But just consider a sea of change that comes our way on which to make decisions in a short space of time. A lot of people leave home, a lot of people start to have serious and meaningful relationships or are planning to enter that space and many are in a process of self-discovery. They have to think about studying further or getting a job. There are so many things on one's plate. There is little time to factor in anything but the necessary.

One of the great things about having avenues for exploration in childhood, that are programmed into the school calendar, is that you have to effectively switch off and you have to do something different, develop another skillset. Whereas everything else post-school is a weighted decision to make – is this activity necessary, is it good for my CV? And so on. It's all so transactional. I think this is where the ludic element, the active fun stuff central to creativity, starts to dwindle. We don't have the time and space for it. We don't make the time and space for it.

And it's not just a feature of early adulthood but a pattern that continues throughout adulthood as life gets more hectic and active, and people become part of the larger workforce and community. And then things change again towards late adulthood. People are increasingly having longer lifespans and you have the situation where people leave the workforce, their lives change and their interactions with the world change and their priorities change. We start to have a much larger older group that are so neglected in terms of their creative and well-being needs.

There is a lot of focus on ageing and physical health as well as ageing in the context of the depletion of cognitive resources. But there is little done on ageing in relation to the arts. We have this sort of fetishisation of age when it comes to creativity. There is a drive in our world to value the first, the youngest. We place so much premium on something quite arbitrary in only focusing on the youngest point in which you do something. That is simply one point in 70, 80, 90 years of somebody's life.

I remember being asked this question once about mathematical creativity and this age curve of originality. I remember hearing from an acquaintance of mine, a mathematician; he said something along the lines of: *Oh my gosh I'm going to reach 30 soon. If I haven't had my original insights by then, I'm screwed.* That is such a weird thing to believe – that the point at which you reach your maximum creativity must be by 30 and after that there is nothing but decline. To put so much premium on one point in your life is misguided. Even if it is in fact completely true that your best ideas will be at 30, there is still a lot of value in your second best and your third best and your fourth best idea.

Christina: *That's fascinating because I am 60 now, and I know my creativity is more important to me than ever.*

I'd like to ask about your inner critic, this voice that goes on in the head, because I think that's interesting in relation to psychology, the old imposter syndrome and what is happening in the brain. Do you get that voice and what does it look like? But also, what do you think is happening for people when that voice comes along? How best to deal with it?

Anna: When we hear about the inner critic, we typically only hear about the super negative, awful voices. I have to say I am quite lucky in that I think I have a couple of inner critics. There are all sorts of things being shot at me at some point. And they are kind of merciless but it's very much a tough love situation. I don't have the kind of voices that will make me feel like I'm worthless or erode my self-esteem. My inner critics are very much the kind of person that I would want to sit and have a conversation with and who would tell me to my face when I'm wrong or being obtuse. I have quite supportive voices. My inner critics are more about grounding me where possible.

Christina: *It sounds like there is more than one?*

Anna: I think of it sometimes as good cop, bad cop, where if one voice is being particularly harsh, *you're such a dummy for thinking that way* or whatever, the other one is like, *well, let's see.* I don't know if that's healthy at all but I tend to think that the voices do their job in that if I am feeling very down and extremely fragile, they don't kick a horse that has fallen. Whereas, when I hear about inner critics that other people have, I find they are harsh, they are lousy. The voice in my head is not just focused on adding fuel to the fire. I tend not to have that purely negative voice, which is why I think I have more than one.

The question though is why it happens. I think self-doubt is always a healthy thing to have. If you don't doubt yourself, this is a real problem because to be so completely assured of one's self as to not think there is any room for growth means that you are entering a very stagnant space and you are going to be an obnoxious human being. Even if some tiny part of you might be right, all the Doubting Toms that exist in your head, whatever form they take for you, serve a purpose, making you understand that there is no way you can understand everything because we are all constructing the world around us as we go through it. We are making meaning out of what we see, and we know that those meanings are not objective in the true sense of the word; they are ever changing. The way I saw something ten days ago is not the same as now.

Look at what's happening now, this important debate about whether statues should be taken down or not. I've walked through such spaces and looked at similar statues and never put much meaning on them, but now I know so much more about the wider context and this is a more interesting predicament to be in. To be able to doubt and reflect on one's assumptions. The ability to doubt is essential for your mind to grow, to be able to consider options beyond the tiny few points of view that you may have access to. It's all about the balance, though. Too much doubt is crippling and too much certainty makes you a closed person. If you are not open, you cannot grow. Certainly not creatively.

Christina: *Oh that makes me feel better because I am always full of doubt. The other side of that is when you do something that is creative in your work; what does it feel like for you when it comes together?*

Have you had moments like that where you have thought: wow, that was great?

Anna: It's interesting because I experience those things, those creative moments of insight in two ways scientifically because my work not only deals with the topic of creativity, I also have to come up with creative ideas, to try to figure out how to study this phenomenon, to figure out the pieces that join the puzzle together. And that requires creative insight. Those creative moments are there, and they are immense when the flashes of genuine insight occur. I also experience moments of creativity on the other side as well, whenever I engage with creative pursuits myself. What's common is the feeling that when you reach that space or when you are in that zone, it just feels like everything fits and jumps into play and in the right place. There is an elegance to it and there is an awareness of the moment. A heightened awareness of the moment. The actual emotional and cognitive spaces merge and in some way, you are looking in from outside yourself on this moment of elegance when it all comes together. There is a beauty to it.

It's something else beholding the process while concurrently being part of it. There is this great quote from Arthur Koestler, who says something along the lines of "the creative moment is where the learner and the teacher are the same person". You become aware of that leap, that semantic and conceptual leap you have made, of the thing that you are beholding. That it's just right.

Christina: *Have you had experience of that in your own work? Can you think of an example where that's actually happened for you?*

Anna: It's interesting because it can happen in small ways and in big ways. I can give you two recent examples. One was while I was editing this volume on the *Cambridge Handbook of the Imagination* (Abraham, 2020). It's an interdisciplinary volume where I have experts from across several disciplines, anthropology, archaeology, neuroscience, philosophy, theology, art and so on, reflect on what the imagination is and how we understand it. I wrote an introductory chapter where the framework for the imagination is discussed and I thought to myself: I must write a conclusion chapter as well. It is not customary to write a concluding chapter in an edited volume, but I felt I needed to do so. I got this diverse set of people together and we produced 47 chapters, and I felt this pressure to bring it all together in the final chapter 48. I needed to have a way of imparting how best to understand the imagination for anyone that has picked up this volume. This is the thing that I want from any book; you've tried to tackle a subject here, what is the take-home message, what do we understand about this? And you can say that we don't understand anything about it. That's fine too. But when I knew that I did understand something more about it, even if I can't quite put my figure on it.

And I realised that what I needed was a metaphor, because we had spent thousands of words talking about what imagination is but we were now lost in the details. And metaphors are very powerful ways to communicate the essence of an idea. So, what is the imagination? It's an absolutely a basic element of our everyday experience. It plays a part in everything we do. It has force. It has flow. And then suddenly I was reminded of the poem about water by Ted Hughes. And I thought to myself – that's it. That's it! The imagination is best conceived of as a force of nature (Saul Bellow characterised it in that way in a novel too). Imagination is like water. And when that insight hit me, it was a key moment where I knew it to be true. That's it. That's exactly it. It is ubiquitous. It flows smoothly. It can be calming and soothing. It can cause storms and destruction. That was a good moment. I think I felt it was a perfect way to end this book. And I use it in the very last paragraph of the book. How the metaphor of water describes the workings of the imagination.

Christina: *That's definitely one of those moments, and it's a powerful metaphor.*

Anna: And as for the second moment – I was at a conference in November, this was pre-lockdown, probably the last conference I attended in person. It was a conference on literature and fiction – one of my key research interests is to understand the difference between reality and fiction – I'd given a talk for this kind of conference a few years previously in Chicago. And basically, there were a lot of literary people in the audience, a few philosophers, and the like. Neuroscientists don't usually get to go anywhere near these types of conferences. But it was because of the work that I had done from a neuroscientific perspective that they were interested in the way I was looking at this question. So, I was invited to this second conference in Paris and when I was proposing the idea of what I was going to write about, I wrote something on the fly without thinking too deeply about it. It was one of those moments where I just did it as a challenge to set myself for future cogitation. I sent the abstract off and six months later, I find that I must do this talk. When the time to prepare finally arrived, I realised I didn't even know how I thought I was going to deliver this lecture. And the pressure mounted because it turned out that my talk was chosen for a keynote lecture. So, I was racking my head thinking, I have to follow my premises and come to my conclusion, but I was lacking the key to it all. And I think about three days before the talk was due, I was still trying to figure it out. How do we implicitly know that fiction is different from reality? And I was sitting in front of my laptop with growing panic, thinking I'm going to make a fool of myself because I don't know the answer. I mean I kind of know, but I can't put it in words. And then I started to think aloud. And then it suddenly came to me. The conceptual insight. That it's about a passive versus and active construction of what we see around us. Fiction is given to us. When I read a book, my attention is being absolutely directed in a particular way. It's like someone leading the orchestra. Reality doesn't have that luxury. My mind has to figure it out by itself. It hit me in an instant. How best to think about the difference and how to conceptualise it.

It was a strange moment. I was racking my head. At one point literally shaking it from side to side. And suddenly, the insight came to me. I'm writing a paper based on that idea now, and hopefully it will come out at some point. Either way it was a great moment. Of relief and joy. It's one of those rare moments where you find that you've had a breakthrough idea. It's a purely theoretical idea but it's exciting, and I hope it will have some utility for researchers.

Christina: *What intrigues me also is what's going on in the brain at that moment too from a neuroscientific point of view. I know the brain is full of little networks and synapses, but that's all. At that moment, what's going on in terms of the science? Is there something different going on??*

Anna: There's a great book called *The Storm of Creativity* (Leski, 2016) which explores the idea that creativity is like a storm in how each of the elements comes together. I would be lying if I said we know exactly how it all works. Like you said – the brain is all synapses and networks. And what we do know is that the same networks are co-opted for a range of different functions and they work in different ways so you have – it's almost banal to say it – but you have a network that is focused towards internal mentation, and a network involved in estimating what is salient in a specific context, and yet another network involved with focused and directed cognitive control. Each of these are dancing with each other if you want. Switching from one to another as the situation demands.

It's very hard to study the creative brain in real time as creative insights cannot be reliably prompted on demand. And as for the neural pathways taken to arrive at the final insight, nobody can really tell you how that happens now. There are people who study processes like the moment of insight, and they find specific neurological signals. It is worth noting though that if you could only see somebody's brain activity and not what they were doing, you would not be able to determine whether the person was undertaking a creativity task or simply mind wandering or carrying out an aesthetic appreciation task. Not without speaking to the person.

Creativity is strongly associated with the moment of having an idea, with this moment of insight that you have, that moment we were talking about earlier when everything comes together. Though there are processes before and after that moment which are also part of the creative process. They involve getting to that insight and working out whether this is a workable idea.

What I hope to do in some of my future work is the focus on not just one but a more detailed and specific neural signature of the creative process. Neuroscience offers interesting insights, not only because it can tell us how something works. It's actually more interesting and more relevant for me to think about how this could be applied. How do the findings from the neuroscientific approach help me understand what a ten-year-old can do to improve her creativity? Is there a certain way of instructing that will lead to a person to have more creativity when grappling with a problem that they need to solve? Can you put yourself in a mental space that will lead to, or is more likely to lead to an insight? And so on. The neuroscientific work is fascinating insofar as it can inform how things work and with that, we know how to do things better.

This is necessary because people are so unaware of their own creativity. I think that is kind of criminal. We need to make people more aware of what it is to be creative. So even that first question that you asked me – what is your earliest memory of being creative? – it would so nice just to get kids to answer that question. What do they understand about their creativity and how does this change as they get older and older and older? I've come across far too many adults who say *I'm not creative* – which to me is such a bizarre thing to say. Because how can you not be? It's a fundamental human capacity.

Christina: *Is it partly related to that moment of letting go of our creativity? It's something that we learn to let go of in the way that you have described and therefore we don't identify with it anymore, as something that's part of us, and we forget to keep it with us, and if it's not present in our lives, in our everyday activity, if it's not for us, then it becomes something difficult. So, I was interested what you are doing in the community to bring that back in for adults, for older people, because as you say, that's crucial and one of the things that we have done with students is to go back to our early memories not necessarily of even being creative but just their own autobiographical stories realising that triggering that memory process seems to give them confidence in their creativity. Perhaps it's just giving them more confidence in their own narrative, their own histories but certainly there seems to be something in that.*

Anna: I think that the telling of a narrative is a constructive process. Drawing back on your memory requires construction as you are seeing and telling a narrative in your own unique way. I can't help but think that has got to feel like a creative moment in some way. Just the telling of it, in and of itself. So that makes lots of sense. As we open up universities post-lockdown, I would start by doing things like focus groups really, because we have little information on what older people feel in terms of their awareness of their creativity. Do they even use the word 'creativity' in the same way as younger people? I would first like to know what our connotations of these terms are. Some of the work that one of my students in Leeds is doing focuses on a comparison of creativity in older and younger adults. In the measures we are looking at, older adults are much more creative than younger adults both in terms of the number of ideas they generate, and the originality of those ideas.

I am fascinated by this because creativity is one of the few abilities that is preserved with age. When studying older people, it's clear that cognitive decline starts in middle age. Cognitive slowness with age is well documented, for instance. But if you look at anything on the side of creativity and imagination, this decline is not very evident at all. There are some aspects of our psychological function then that are quite impervious to decline. When you examine neurological patients with different types of brain damage, for instance, it's not that they are simply worse on every aspect of complex human function. A far more nuanced picture surfaces. In some cases, such patients exhibit better performance than their neurotypically matched controls because, in some specific ways, the altered brain bestows advantages for aspects of creativity. Some creative operations benefit from greater distractibility, for instance, as they prevent one from sauntering down the same well-trodden path all the time. It allows one to try something different.

So, my experience with older people has really made me realise how we know really very little about their creative process. I asked my doctoral student what it's like to test them. And she said they are the most joyous group of people to test. When we examined the types of ideas they generated, we noticed that when you looked at the strategies the older people were drawing on, there is a real difference in the degree of detail, the practicality and so on. We used the alternate uses task where we ask people to generate as many new uses as they can for common objects. What are the unusual uses one can use a brick for and so on? Older samples lean on their abundant practical knowledge, much of which is autobiographical. So, they would say: *Well, I remember when I was younger this object was there*. Something about the task revived their early memories. They probably hadn't thought about that use for that object for a while but this fun creativity task jogs specific memories and stimulates the mind still further. I would like to gain a clearer understanding of what kind of creative pursuits they do. We don't really have a sense of what's important to sustain the creative impulse of older people. Is sociability an important component? Are there other factors involved? There is some work, for instance, that shows that wisdom increases with age. Perhaps that ties to creativity as well. I need to find out more and I need to with more age-based charities.

With the endowment that comes with my new job is the opportunity to direct the funds to do community outreach-based work. I've never been in a position as an academic where you don't have to write a funding bid to do this sort of work. I am lucky to have found a position in the institution where a giant in the world of creativity, E Paul Torrance, worked for several decades. He left a sizeable amount of money as an endowment to UGA to be used towards ends that promote creativity. It can be community-based and need not be tied to an academic publication or another pure research-based outcome. I've never been in that position before. So, I aim to take a life-span approach to community outreach in service of creativity, and part of that approach is connecting with all the communities involved. Another PhD student of mine is studying creativity in younger people, and her work involves estimating the influence of individual versus environmental predictors of creative potential. It is a longitudinal study where young people between 14 and 18 years are studied and then followed up two years later. One of the most stable findings we have found is that, over and above every other factor, the trait of openness to experience is the most robust predictor of creative potential. The question that arises then is whether this personality trait can be encouraged and enhanced. Will openness to experience be an important predictor of creativity in older samples as well?

Christina:	*And when you say 'openness to experience', do you mean being open to experiences that are different to the ones that you would normally engage with in your daily life, that are outside your comfort zone?*
Anna:	Openness reflects many things. The ability to go beyond your comfort zone and try something new. Fantasy proneness. Intellectual or artistic engagement with aesthetic experience. And so on. Such findings on openness make me consider what we can do to encourage openness. Can we set up stimulating cultural festivals to enable that, for instance? I would be looking to work together with artists and like-minded individuals to really bring something of that sort together. A festival of imaginative ideas, so to speak. Even if we could set up spaces where people can create work together, that would be a big achievement. And now that everyone can speak to one another with video calling despite being miles apart, such avenues may provide a great opportunity to give people who are less mobile the opportunity to connect together. People who are far away from one another connect to engage with a collective aim in mind that can be community based.

We will always need creative solutions to overcome our big problems in the world. And we need people to feel empowered and aware of their own creativity and capabilities to be in the position to be solution makers. We need to connect people and get people to communicate well to build supportive communities. We did a bunch of community-based activities when I was a young teen as part of our school activities. Even at the time I knew this was a special way of doing things. If there is a way to make things more harmonious and make people more understanding of each other, the best way to do it is to get them to come face to face and work towards a common aim.

I remember when I was 13, part of one of the initiatives in school was helping kids who came from poorer communities. Their parents were the service staff – cleaners and cooks in the school. Their kids were attending the local school, which was free but did have proper instruction. So, we tutored these kids for a couple of months in maths and English – 13-year-olds teaching these 10-year-olds. It was such fun. First of all because we were all at this silly age and you are just having so much giggly fun. All of us could see that these younger students were so bright. They might have been poor at reading or maths but were certainly no less creative than us in any sense of the word. It was a simple initiative to break down class barriers, even if only temporarily.

And really made me understand later how fortunate I was by mere accident of birth. And I also felt so useful then as a 13-year-old kid. I was of use to others.

So, I want to foster community-based initiatives where people from different backgrounds within communities meet and work on something together. Such interactions are particularly fun, valuable and memorable when the common aim involves creativity.

Postscript

> the imagination … it's like water … it's ubiquitous, it flows smoothly, it can be calming and it can be the cause of storms, it can cause destruction. … It's about how the metaphor of water describes the imagination.
>
> *(Anna Abraham)*

At the time of writing, I was reading Maggie O'Farrell's novel *Hamnet* (2020) about the life of Shakespeare's son in the sixteenth century in which she writes: "every life has its kernel, its hub, its epicentre from which everything else flows out, to which everything else returns" (p. 8). These words make me pause and reflect on the source of Anna's creative flow and consider whether the values of inclusivity and community mindedness which seem to drive much of Anna's work are related to Anna's wish to honour both her family and the community in India that was supportive of her creative and academic talents when she was growing up. But also, to the frustration she felt when she struggled to find suitable outlets where she could pursue her love of theatre and performance in parallel with academic studies at University. It seems to me that as a result of these conflicting experiences, Anna now wants to create a world full of creative opportunity, accessible to all.

And so, Anna's description of water as a way of conceiving the imagination seems to be exactly right, because the imagination is always with us, coursing through the hinterlands of our mind like an unseen river ebbing and flowing, a constant companion that helps us to interpret our everyday lives. And of course, it would be simple if this creative current continued unimpeded but as Anna's story reminds us, setbacks, doubts and feelings of uncertainty are part of the human experience from which we change and grow. Like boulders found littering the riverbed, it is these obstacles that have the potential to create unexpected new tributaries, moments of gushing, bubbling up, and ripples in our lives and our creativity. From this perspective, these setbacks and diversions are, Anna seems to be saying, as much a part of our creativity as its unimpeded flow.

Since those early days, Anna has artfully steered her way around any boulders she has encountered to redirect her energies into an inspiring and successful academic life, where she has been able to extend our understanding of what creativity means in terms of its neuroscientific and psychological concepts and principles, and also offered practical solutions to the problem of improving access to creativity for all.

Bibliography

Abraham, A. (Ed.) (2020). *The Cambridge handbook of the imagination*. Cambridge University Press. ISBN: 9781108429245.

Abraham, A. G. (2015). Gender and creativity: An overview of psychological and neuroscientific literature. *Brain Imaging and Behaviour*. ISSN: 1931-7565. https://doi.org/10.1007/s11682-015-9410-8. http://eprints.leedsbeckett.ac.uk/1540/

Leski, K. (2016). *The storm of creativity*. The MIT Press. ISBN: 978-0-262-53949-4.

O' Farrell, M. (2020). *Hamnet*. Tinder Press.

WHAT IS CREATIVITY?

A Response to Anna Abraham

Christina Reading

What is creativity? Answering this question is a challenge, because despite the long history of theorists and writers and artists that can be traced, at least as far back to the writings of Plato over 2,000 years ago, people have tried to explain and define its characteristics but creativity remains a nebulous, mysterious and pondered about process (Vernon, 1970; Sesonske, 1965; Runco & Garrett, 2012; Glück, Ernst & Unger, 2002; Ford & Harris,1992; Harrington 2018; Warner, 2018; Leski, 2020; hooks, 1995).

It is not my intention to rehearse these endeavours to frame and conceptualise creativity here, except perhaps to note that some of the women writers whose work I have encountered recently have used metaphor to represent the process. Kyna Leski (2020) for instance, refers to creativity as a storm: "the creative process is bigger than you. It's like a storm that slowly begins to gather and take form until it overtakes you – if you are willing to let it" (Leski, 2020, p. xxiv). And Marina Warner (2018) evokes a Seamus Heaney phrase the "trawl net of the mind" from the preface to the magazine *The Crane Bag Book of Irish Studies* (1977–1981) as a phrase to describe acts of visual imagination and how to describe how the 'treasures" in the mind are retrieved during the creative process (Warner, 2018, p. 252). She writes:

> the metaphor of the trawl net does not forget that the mind's retrievals and hauls are only ever partial: every fishing community knots specific nets for certain catches, with meshes at regular intervals, with twine of different thickness and gauges. All nets have holes and every attempt at capture is accompanied by loss, just as language proliferates but never suffices to cover all of experience. Something will always elude capture.
>
> *(Warner, 2018, p. 251)*

DOI: 10.4324/9781003286042-3

Jess, my collaborator in this book, conjured up the image of a 'magic cloud' to describe her creativity in our last book, whereas for me creativity often feels like a puzzle to be solved, a process in which I use trial and error to work out which pieces fit together in order to produce a coherent image or piece of writing (Reading & Moriarty, 2020, p. 48). During my conversation with Anna about the nature of creativity, she used the metaphor of water to evoke the imagination, and these metaphors, whilst effective in invoking the mystery that is creativity, underline the fact that the exact workings and a fixed definition of creativity remain obscure, opaque, and that it is a process, not always adequately described by words alone. And I reflect that for me, creativity is an embodied experiencing hovering between thinking, looking, imagining, feeling and doing, guided always by an instinct that often overrules any rational plan that I might have for a piece of work and characterised by periods of frustration, boredom and rare moments of satisfaction when a piece of work I make offers me something back. It starts a conversation and seems to take on a life of its own. Certainly, I know too that my creativity flourishes with the encouragement of others. It is supported and encouraged by other activities central to my life – talking to other artists, walking with friends and family and swimming in the cold English sea.

And given this history and complexity, I wonder how to navigate a path through this topic in a way that is meaningful to me within the context of my intention to gather stories of women's experience of creativity in this book. The traditional academic route would be to start with a literature review based on weeks of work, trawling the records of the university library, but given that I no longer work in academia and no longer have access to the library system, this option doesn't align with the reality of where I write from, which is, as a practising artist working alongside but outside HE. I briefly consider persuading Jess to lend me her library card, but instinctively feel it's important not to alter or shut out the perspective that I bring to the project, nor involve my friend in an act of subterfuge.

In the end, I wondered what would happen if I decided to take the same approach to researching this question as I do to my creative work, where I have "adopted an approach to making that uses what is nearer at hand, easily available to me and already part of my life" (Reading, 2015, p. 34). Since leaving art college I, like many women artists, faced the challenge of producing work alongside a busy working and family life. But the artworks I made do not deny these circumstances, and instead sought to draw inspiration from them. This decision was (and still is) driven primarily by a desire to make work, whether that is writing or art, that stems from my personal experience. I am a daughter, sister, mother, friend and partner, and these relationships are central to my experience. They matter to me. I am also a person who has had cancer twice, feel lucky to be alive and fragile, tentative in the thoughts and emotions I have about the future, but I don't always want to make work that draws on this aspect of my experiences; although it's part of my experience, it's not its entirety. Instinctively, I feel I don't want to offer a perspective that feigns an objective assessment of what others have said on this question: What is creativity? All I hope to do is write about the ideas of other artists and writers as they inform my own search for understanding this topic.

Hence my review is based on the materials I have gathered from home, the studio, friends, Google searches and my own practice. In other words, I intend to offer a path that is personal, reflecting the reality of where I write from. Academia, I fear, will shudder, but I decide that literature reviews offer only a subjective and partial, incomplete review of a topic, written from the standpoint of where you exist in the world, and what power (access to resources, connections and knowledge) you have at your disposal. I choose to believe that my power to shed some light on the question I address in this chapter and my ability to effect change, to offer insights into this topic will come from my creativity as well as my situation. My endeavour is guided by curiosity, and my hope is that I can find clues into some of the complexities of navigating this terrain using this personal approach. And I do this in the hope of encouraging other women to speak of and share their diversities of understanding and experiences of creativity. To write and make from their personal perspectives of the world and to value these contributions is important and significant to the unfolding story of what creativity is.

Back in the studio I share with other artists, my curiosity is stirred by a neglected text tucked away on a musty shelf in the shared kitchen: a remnant, I speculate, from one of my fellow artist's student days. It's a collection of writings edited by Alexander Sesonske: *What Is Art? Aesthetic Theory from Plato to Tolstoy* (1965). The book boldly claims to provide a gathering of some of the key classical writing about the arts and aesthetics. The text starts with the writings of Plato (428–348 BC) with contributions from key thinkers from the 18th and 19th centuries such as Georg Wilhelm Friedrich Hegel (1770–1831), Friedrich Nietzsche (1844–1900) and Leo Tolstoy (1828–1910).

I am interested in Sesonske's claim that he regards Plato's writings as the keystone for subsequent discourse about creativity and underlines the fact that creativity is not just a contemporary concern but is an issue and question that has deep roots.

The importance of Plato in this history stems not merely from the fact that he is the first western writer to discuss art objects and artists seriously, analytically, and in generic terms – questioning both the meaning of aesthetic terms in common use and common-sense beliefs about the arts – but that in the half dozen or so dialogues in which he touches, briefly or at length on aesthetic questions, he explores the whole field. He does not, of course, clearly formulate all, or even many, of the problems of aesthestics – but he suggests then all, as well as the answers which are elaborated through subsequent Western thought.

(Sesonske, 1965, p. xiv)

My eye lands on a definition of creativity offered by Plato:

There is creative activity, which as you know is complex and manifold. All that causes the passage of non-being into being is a 'poesy' or a creation, and all processes of the arts are creative, and all the masters of the Arts are poets or creators.

Plato, Symposium (9201c–212a) in Sesonske, A (1965), p. 40; Socrates during a conversation about the nature of beauty with *Agathan*

(written by Plato, 201c–212a)

Here creativity is posited as a multifaceted process that ushers in new ideas, new ways of seeing, new ways of being, new ways of doing that bring forward and present something to the world that hasn't quite been there before – processes that reshape what has been. Despite the chasm of historical time, I acknowledge this explanation as a precedent. But perhaps it makes me wonder about what personal definitions of creativity the women I will talk to during this research might offer – how their accounts might extend, complicate or differ from this ancient characterisation.

Additionally, Plato's assertion in this definition that it is the arts that have the most to teach us about the nature of creativity because all its methods are potentially creative reassures me that my focus and interest in this book on what women writers and artists have to say about their creativity is fertile territory for understanding this topic, indeed, that such conversations are integral to it. Hence, whilst I acknowledge that it's possible to be creative in all aspects of life, my interest in the artistic activity of women seems a good place to start. And I feel excited by the potential insights into this territory that will be gained by our talking to women artists about their creativity and their processes.

But it does not escape my attention that of the 29 contributors to the Sesonske collection, are men, reflecting the historic silence and invisibility of women in this discourse. Nevertheless, I skim the book's contents, trying to pick up clues about what these classical texts might have to say about creativity. I am looking for a starting point, a route into this discourse.

However, even as I do this, I can see Jess's sceptical face and quizzical eyebrow raising the question of why resurrect the thinking of these privileged white men, why give a platform here to these ideas? What about all the contemporary writers, especially the women, who have things to say about this subject? And what about the other traditions? The non-Western points of view? And indeed, perhaps this ancient past will be too distant for me to find any connection to present-day thinking and questions about women's creativity, but whilst acknowledging these limitations and this risk, all I can say in defence is that it feels important to acknowledge where ideas about creativity have occurred in history and find the links to the present day.

> Feminism has never been the pure and innocent other of a guilty and evil patriarchy. It has always been obliged to use the masters' tools to destroy his house and has done so in the full knowledge this this complicity with its corruption and contamination is itself an action against metaphysics.
>
> *(Colebrook, 2000, p. 3)*

And I reflect that all women artists and writers seeking to contribute their voices to this discourse on artistic creativity are faced with the problem of working with the ideas and symbols laid down by earlier writers and artists, often male, whilst also asserting their own voices to create spaces to allow distinctly feminist views of creativity to emerge. My perspective is that a feminist needs to both acknowledge these traditions and histories where they are relevant to her concerns and speak the relevance of the issues raised for women, to also feel free to make use of and reclaim these ideas and legacies, make them their own. To be inspired by this past in its dialogue with the present day. Of course, this means that feminist perspectives are to some extent sabotaged by the pre-existing discourses arising from patriarchy, but discussions of women's creativity exist in relation to and emerge from these discourses.

I turn to Sesonske's editorial summation of these classical texts, and I am struck by his argument that the question: *What Is Art?* is not really a question but a series of questions that different thinkers from the ancients to modern times (pre-20th century) have tried to answer different aspects of in different ways (Sesonske, 1965, xi). Whilst some writers have focused on what an art object is and questions of form, styles and genre's purpose and function and the like, Sesonske reminds us that the classical world, led by Plato (428–348 BC) focused on the ideas of art object as imitation or mimesis (Plato, *Republic X* (595–608b) in Sesonske, 1965, pp. 228–238-) and questions of the beauty of art objects (Plato, *Symposium*, 9201c–212a in Sesonske, 1965, pp. 38–44). According to Plato, the idea is the most valuable and important kind of creative act; others may imitate (mimesis) or make use of the original idea by making copies, but this is regarded as an inferior skill. And crucially only God is capable of this original creative activity; artists merely mimic or make use of the ideas that they find in what God has made, in nature.

Whilst other writers dealt with how the viewer engages with the object and the nature of that encounter, with questions of the imagination and the emotions of the viewer at the fore. Sesonske notes that by the 18th century: "attention focuses upon the experience and response of the viewer; the art object is treated as instrumental to this response" (Sesonske, 1965, p. xv) led by writer Joseph Addison (1672–1719) and his essay on the "pleasures of the imagination" (Addison in Sesonske 1965, pp. 113–118). Considering the question from the perspective of the experience of the view rather than the nature of the art object was also the subject of Edmund Burke's (1728–1797) 1756 essay, 'A Philosophical Inquiry into the Origin of Our Ideas of the Sublime and the Beautiful' (Burke in Sesonske, 1965, pp. 138–154). The third set of questions places the artists centre stage and have addressed to what extent art is to do with the artist's intention and creative process, asking whether it matters what is produced or what is made. This includes the discussion of the artist's inspiration and imagination. There is a concern for the personality and character of the artist. For instance, in his essay 'What Is Art?' Leo Tolstoy (1828–1910) (Tolstoy, 1898, in Sesonske 1965, pp. 406–418) regards Art as "one of the means of intercourse between man and man" (Tolstoy, 1898 in Sesonske, 1965, p. 410) and that "by means of words, a man transits his thoughts to another, by means of art, he transits his feelings" (Tolstoy, 1898 in Sesonske, 1965, p. 410). In other words, it's how an artist expresses themself that is central to the artistic and creative process. And as Sesonske continues, answers to these questions relate to other variable elements in our society, to education, to culture, economics, politics, science, and the like (Sesonske, 1965, pp. xi–xvi). It is clearly knotty territory and raises additional questions for me about who the arbitrator and judge of all these different facets of the Arts and creativity – the expert, the art institutions, everybody, women, ourselves? Sesonske concludes: "It is as much a history of the emergence of new questions as the formulation of new answers. And here, as elsewhere, the greatest ferment often occurs when somebody discovers a new question rather than answering an old one" (Sesonske, 1965, p. xiv).

What I learn from this discussion is that the question of what creativity is raises a myriad of questions and that writers past and present have been concerned with different aspects and fragments of it, each offering at best a partial insight, a piece of the puzzle rather than the whole. I understand from this discussion that I will not find a single definitive and neat answer to the question of what creativity is; instead, I must think more precisely about the questions that concern me in relation to this topic and frame my definition within this context.

Sesonske's discussion and insights about these ancient texts help me frame my concept of creativity for this book because I realise whilst acknowledging that there are other aspects of creativity to be investigated and other perspectives on this topic, the task before me is to investigate the question – *What is creativity?* – from the perspective of women's experience of creativity. And the absence of women in his text reminds me once again of the importance of ensuring the research for this book contributes to the unfolding story of women's creativity. I am interested in what women have to say about their creativity and creative processes. And the specificity of that seems to me to be a potentially much trickier but more exciting question. In this endeavour, I realise that I am not seeking a definitive answer to this question but simply wish to gather glimpses and fragments into the nature of women's creative practice in the hope that this will provide insights into the nature of women's experience of creativity. This work will help me to provide a platform for the diversity of those experiences and consider ways in which women's creativity can be encouraged and supported.

But whatever mysteries remain to be unravelled in our understanding of the artistic creation process in relation to women, I agree with Sesonske (1965) in so far as he argues that:

> theory follows practice, in that theoretical questions initially arise in the context of some practical encounter in the world. Some data of experience. The basic data in this field are the myriad occurrences of song, dance, painting, sculpture, architecture, poetry, drama produced and responded to with a frequency, regularity and insistence which marks a universal and fundamental aspect of human culture.
>
> *(Sesonske, 1965, p. xii)*

In other words, all the creative acts that individual women artist and writers undertake in their practical work matter, and from this work, theoretical ideas are developed. I take from this the idea that ideas trying to account for women's creativity come first and foremost from understanding these processes, but it's also about the myriad of questions that arise from this effort, including (but not limited to):

- What do women artists choose to bring into being through their creativity?
- What personal definitions of creativity do women offer?
- What do they choose to create/make/do and why?
- What ways of seeing the world does women's creativity offer?
- Why is creativity valued, and why does it matter to women?
- Why do women strive to develop it and wield it despite the challenges of juggling a personal/professional life and how is this supported and encouraged – by themselves and the people around them, their creative community?

These questions clarify for me that in this book we are concerned with gathering stories from women as a starting point for understanding the nature of their experiences and addressing the questions their endeavours raise. And we will follow the lead provided by the women we talk to in this book to see what new questions emerge from this discourse about how creativity is viewed and how it can be encouraged and supported. These are the inquiries that this research will address, and the pursuit of them will lead hopefully to yet unknown questions coming to light: an end that aims to lay down stepping-stones for further research.

These aims in relation to the question of what creativity is having been defined, I turn next to talk about the methods we will use in this book. The time spent reading these ancient ideas has reminded me that I enjoy history and that my inclination in my writing and in painting is to seek inspiration from the past, to see what resonates in the present moment. And whilst I am pottering around the kitchen, Melvyn Bragg's programme, *In Our Times*, comes on to Radio 4. He's talking about Plato's *Gorgias*, billed as the most personal of Plato's dialogues, in which he examines the values that led to the execution of his mentor, Socrates. I listen, thinking that I might learn something to flesh out my minimal understanding of Plato's life and work. I take from the conversation between Melvyn Bragg and his radio guests that Plato devoted his writings to the exploration of philosophical issues, posing questions about how we ought to live and what kind of people we should strive to be. To test out his ideas and to get to the truth of these matters, Plato created a series of speeches or dialogues between characters. And in one of these, Plato's *Gorgias*, he argued against the use of rhetoric as a conversational form, suggesting that although a powerful method of persuasion, it wasn't a method suited to seeking the truth. Instead, he argued that dialogue or conversation was best placed to get to the heart of these issues because it allowed speakers to come together for the common purpose of exploring a topic, creating the potential for reciprocity and equality in the discussion. I take from this that Plato favoured friendly, open, supportive discourse, rather than one based on the skills of individual orators. And Plato favoured this form because he didn't want to tell people what to think, but to allow them to come to their own conclusions on the ideas and topics explored in the dialogues. Even in Plato's time, supportive conversation, as Jess and I have advocated in previous research and will use as a way of gathering stories of women's experience of creativity for this book, eclipses other forms of dialogue as a way of understanding the nature of experience. And I must acknowledge that the method we will use occurs within the context of this ancient history.

I am pleased to listen to this debate bubbling away in the background because it shows me that the conversational method that we have chosen for this book to investigate questions of creativity is a form associated with a search for truth, a method that tries to tease out knowing whilst allowing for inconsistencies and differences of opinions to co-exist in the pursuit of some common ground: a method that doesn't impose its view of creativity on others but allows readers the space to consciously reflect on their beliefs and understanding of their creativity. I find this method creates a space in which through dialogue new ideas can emerge, contributing to a personal discourse on creativity that each reader can devise for themselves. Jess and I offer insights into our own thinking and the reflections and ideas of the women we are talking with but hope that these will inspire new thinking and reflection in each reader, enabling them to identify a model of creativity that works for them. And in our conversations with women artists about their creativity, we encourage a self-conscious act of reflection that echoes the form Plato advocated. In other words, a crucial aspect of our method includes an open, friendly, supportive natural discourse between women rather than an interrogation of women. The dialogue that Jess and I seek to encourage in our method is straightforward, meaningful and attempts to allow all involved to speak plainly and honestly about their experiences within the context of a supported guided conversation.

Conclusion

I reach the end of this chapter clearer about the definitions and methods that will guide this research. Firstly, I conclude that, yes, history – other writers and artists – offers us definitions and explanations of creativity that contribute to our understanding of that experience, but ultimately, I believe that no one definition can grasp what creativity is because this is rooted in the lived experience of women. In other words, this project values personal definition of creativity and the aim of this project is simply to allow the cacophony of the individual voices of women to be heard. Hence the aim of our project is to create a space for feminist voices to emerge – to offer ideas and thinking about creativity that stem from the experience of women artists and writers, asking questions about what it is like to be a creative woman now, to live in these shoes. To reflect on what the women's stories we gather have to say to us, to the ancient past, to the history of discourse on creativity.

And if the story of what creativity is, is in fact the history of the questions posed about creativity as I have discussed, then Anna Abraham's research points us to the importance of the new questions being asked in the world of neuroscience about how the brain works during creative tasks: questions facilitated by technological advances in imaging technology that lead to the detailed study and collection of information on the processes in the neural circuits and pathways of the brain; it's certainly fascinating stuff. But as Anna says, understanding these mechanics is helpful only insofar as they raise further questions about how best to apply these discoveries so that creativity can be supported and encouraged for all. Her concern as shown by the earlier conversation between us is with how creativity can be applied in the world.

How it can be used to solve the pressing problems that society must address such as climate change and managing artificial intelligence.

Anna's words also remind us that being creative is a "fundamental human capacity" and that there is value in supporting people's creativity from all ages and communities. But also, how culture and lack of education can hinder women's opportunities to be creative and dent self-confidence so that consequentially dealing with self-doubt and developing a constructive relationship to our inner critics is a crucial part of developing women's creative capacity.

And I would argue that the strategy we use in this book, of gathering and sharing women's individual insights, is a means to empower women, can help them see their differences as well as crossovers with the experiences of other women.

Creative Task: You Are Creative

I describe creativity as a 'puzzle to be solved'; Jess refers to it as 'a magic cloud'. Reflect on the following questions with a friend.

- What is your personal experience of being creative?
- Which image represents your personal view of creativity?
- Draw a picture and/or write a few words about this image.
- Share your image and description with your friend.

Bibliography

Bragg, M. (2020). *Plato's Gorgias* Radio 4. https://www.bbc.co.uk/programmes/m0011rzy

Colebrook, C. (2000). Introduction. In I. Buchanan, & C. Colebrook (Eds.), *Deleuze and feminist theory* (pp. 1–13). Edinburgh University Press.

Ford, D. Y., & Harris, J. J. (1992). The elusive definition of creativity. *The Journal of Creative Behavior, 26*(3), 186–198. https://doi.org/10.1002/j.2162-6057.1992.tb01175.x

Glück, J., Ernst, R., & Unger, F. (2002). How creatives define creativity: Definitions reflect different types of creativity. *Communications Research Journal*. https://doi.org/10.1207/S15326934CRJ14015

Harrington, D. M. (2018). On the usefulness of "value" in the definition of creativity: A commentary. *Creativity Research Journal, 30*(1), 118–121. https://doi.org/10.1080/10400419.2018.1411432

Hederman, M. P., & Kearney, R. (1982). *The crane bag book of Irish studies 1977-1981*. Blackwater Press. ISBN 10: 090547113X. ISBN 13: 9780905471136

hooks, b. (1995). Women artists: The creative process. In Robinson, H. (Ed), *Feminism art theory: An anthology, 1968-2000* (pp. 635–641). Blackwell Publishers Ltd 2001.

Leski, K. (2020). *The storm of creativity*. The Massachusetts Institute of Technology (MIT) Press.

Merleau-Ponty, M. (2012). *Phenomenology of perception*. Routledge.

Panofsky, E. (1943). *Albrecht Durer* (Vol. 2). Oxford University Press.

Reading, C. (2015). Re-presenting melancholy: Figurative art and feminism. D Phil Thesis The University of Brighton in collaboration with the University of the Creative Arts.

Reading, C., & Moriarty, J. (2020). *Walking for creative recovery: A handbook for creatives, with insights and ideas for supporting your creative life*. Triarchy Press.

Runco, M. A., & Garrett, J. J. (2012). The standard definition of creativity. *Creativity Research Journal*, 24(1), 92–96. https://doi.org/10.1080/10400419.2012.650092

Sesonske, A. (1965). *What is art? Aesthetic Theory from Plato to Tolstoy*. Oxford University Press.

Vernon, P. E. (1970). *Creativity*. Penguin Books Ltd.

Warner, M. (2018). *Forms of enchantment: Writings on art and artists*. Thames and Hudson.

2

REAL AND IMAGINED EXPLORATIONS OF SELF

A Conversation with Katarina Ranković

Christina Reading

FIGURE 2.1 Pseudo (2018). 6 minutes 18 seconds. Video.

Katarina is a performance and text-based artist addressing the question of personhood through the guise of fictional characters, using filmed and also live performance (see Figure 2.1). As a Serb born in Yorkshire, raised in Norway, both the theory and practice of Katarina's work originates (she says) from the daily necessity of inhabiting and switching between [her] many selves.

Currently a PhD student at Goldsmiths University, she regularly exhibits, performs, publishes, and lectures on her work at a diverse range of public

DOI: 10.4324/9781003286042-4

venues. These include Nottingham Contemporary, Tate Modern, Bermondsey Art Project Space, the Cockpit Theatre, Somerset House, Camden People's Theatre, Lewisham Arthouse, Refinery29, NOWNESS (short film commission), Birmingham City University and Crypt Gallery. Katarina is the recipient of the Golden Aesop Grand Prix in Contemporary Art at the 24th Biennial of Humour and Satire (2019) and the Refinery29 Artist Vision Award (2017).

Katarina's work first came to my attention via an old friend, Ken Turner, who now runs a contemporary art gallery in South London called the Tension Fine Art Gallery (https://www.tensionfineart.co.uk/), where Katarina recently had an exhibition of her film performance work.

Before the interview, I spend the morning online watching a series of Katarina's fascinating, absorbing and sometimes unsettling films. Inhabiting an array of fictional characters, her body and her imagination fuse to reveal characters whose voices, somatic gestures, social and cultural backgrounds and clothes vary depending on the story they narrate. I particularly love the film entitled 'The Widow' (2014), where a demure, well-dressed woman sits on a high stool and coolly declares, "and that's when the dissecting began, he was cut into two, then in four … you know how it goes on … halves and halves and halves until he became an atom, that's what happened to my husband". In 'Computerised Existence' (2015), a film about living in a world surrounded by new technology, "everything is made of pixels; I can feel them waving between my toes like grass", declares the character, as if in a trance.

Whether these performances and other text-based works are different articulations of herself or speak of the lives of others, the connections seem to me to speak about the possibility of transformation. Katarina explores herself and her identity/ies through the fictional characters she performs and offers a voice for the different aspects of the self. The films showcase a series of "improvised performances where the artist uses her voice and sometimes her body to shape shift into a Frankenstein collage of gesticulation, accents and mannerisms that she picks from the people that interest her, be they fictitious or real" (Ranković, 2016). It is an entertaining, disconcerting, and yet ultimately empowering practice.

In our conversation, Katarina tells us her story of how she used her practice to recover her confidence and find her voice as an artist and of the importance of having a trusted advisor you can turn to in difficult times to help you through. In Katarina's case, it was her parents, with her father advising her early on that university would not teach her to be an artist, because she already was an artist. This helped her to realise that she didn't need to fit into some preconceived notion of what an artist is or what an artist does, and slowly Katarina came to trust herself and her own unique vision with which she now illuminates the world. *Just be yourself* is her message to other artists who might be experiencing a loss of confidence. *It is enough.*

Christina: *Perhaps you would begin by telling me a little about your work?*

Katarina: I also went to Central St Martins and did my MA there, two years ago now, so I come from a Fine Art background, and I suppose I was drawn to study that subject because I am working in vastly different media. I would say what unites everything – whether I work in film, performance or text – is that I am a storyteller, so my work is very narrative based. I'm writing a novel, but I am also doing performance videos, and I have a very focused drawing practice although I haven't drawn in years. So, I work in a lot of different media. I am a writer, then I do film and then I do theatre, but I'm always telling stories through these different media, and I'm often taking on different characters. I like to imagine I am inhabiting different personas through the work.

Christina: *That's interesting. Have you always worked in that way? What was it like when you were young?*

Katarina: I can't remember when I was not being an artist. Some people don't like that term, but I call myself an artist. And I think in the beginning it was much more drawing. I was constantly drawing. I do have an early memory, I think I was five and, well, my parents are quite artistic people. My dad was a painter and he obviously always had that stuff around, and so I was very naturally picking it up, but I remember once doing something extremely disciplined for a five year old. I had a piece of paper and there was a doll in front of me, one of my dolls, and my dad said *now draw the doll* and the first thing he said to do was keep looking, and I remember feeling annoyed because he kept interrupting my drawing to tell me to keep looking at the doll. But there was also something a bit exciting about it because very quickly, even as a five-year-old, I was seeing the doll in a new way, and my dad taught me something really wonderful in that moment and that was that we don't really see the world in front of us. It was quite a philosophical experience, and it was a bit scary because I was suddenly seeing the doll as I'd never seen it before, and I realised, I'm not seeing the things in front of me.

Christina: *Do you remember that thought landing in your mind at that age?*

Katarina: Yes, I do I remember feeling unsettled and partially annoyed because my dad purposely kept talking to me, *Look at the doll, look again, look at the doll*, but also unsettled by really seeing the object transfigure in front of me and then going back to my daily life afterwards and being wary of everything. It was a lesson in perception, I guess.

Christina: *It sounds like quite a transformative experience.*

Katarina: I think one thing that really rubbed off was how enjoyable a disciplined activity can be.

Christina: *It sounds as if your parents were quite formative in your early attempts to be creative. What about schools or other influences?*

Katarina: Your questions got me thinking a lot. My dad was teaching me to look. At school, my friends were teaching me to draw but they were very much – *here's a circle for a head, here is the body* – and I drew my Barbie in the way that dad had taught me and I remember taking it to school and showing it to my friends and they said it was rubbish, probably because the lines were sketchy. It didn't follow an iconography that they were familiar with. My dad was trying to teach me a realistic way of looking, but they really liked these sort of stylised dolls, iconographical cartoon drawings. So, I remember feeling very insecure, trying to forget what my dad had taught me and learn from them, this popular style of drawing and bringing that home to my father. He was so dismayed that they had ruined my drawing. I remember early on this sort of fight almost between my dad trying to teach me his way of seeing and to open my mind to the play of perception and letting me to go to school and get all these influences at school that he thought were sort of damaging.

Christina: *What about teachers? Anybody else that helped or hindered you?*

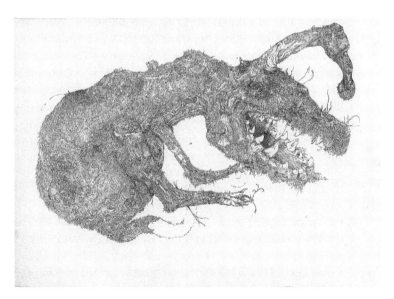

FIGURE 2.2   Rocket Dog (2014). Ink on paper. 420 × 297 mm.

Katarina: I didn't have a particularly good relationship with teachers. In the early days there were some teachers who noticed that my writing style was interesting or creative, but I learnt to distrust teachers early on because in primary school I had some difficulties. I had a bit of bullying going on and I was being accused of things I didn't do, and the teachers actually thought I did these things. I really learnt to distrust adults that weren't my parents but the reason I mention that is because in a way my art was something I could really consult for support. It was something the teachers couldn't take away from me, so if ever I had any trouble, I would immediately seek solace from writing something or drawing something, and then it would sort of block out the world.

Christina: *That's quite powerful, that gathering of your sense of yourself through what you are doing, a very powerful reinforcing strategy.*

Katarina: In a way it was the feeling that I had opponents in life that reinforced this need to have this thing that was mine. That nobody could touch.

Christina: *When you were doing this writing and this drawing, were there particular themes that you addressed?*

Katarina: I think I was extremely interested in drawing people, and I had an extraordinarily strong interest in artificial intelligence as a little girl. I wanted to make a robot, and so I was often drawing engineering type drawings. I didn't know anything about engineering but through my drawing, I liked to have a mix between the organic looking, animal world but also merging with the machine and often beings that I felt I could be, something that in my mind I idealised, and I would feel empowered by imagining (see Figure 2.2). Another thing I wanted to mention was that when I was about eight years old, these works, whether they were writing or drawing, started to take a chronicling nature so I started to write my age on my drawings, imagining that archaeologists would find my drawings, that they would want to know about me. I started writing diaries and I still write diaries. I have books and books of them. You may find this with other people that you interview, this need to create some sort of space where you can create or discover yourself.

Christina: *No, that makes perfect sense. In those diaries, was there a combination of writing and drawing together? Was that your way of exploring difficulties that you encountered? Or was it just a way of having fun?*

Katarina: It was both, I think. One of the strengths of art, of what it can do for the artist at least, is to harness something troubling and then turn it into something you can control or modify, or make fun of, so for me it was a little bit compulsive. For example, if I got told off in a classroom, I would suddenly feel incredibly embarrassed at my desk, and I would grab a pen and just doodle, and immediately it was like a salve. I felt like I was investing myself in the page and there was nobody else on the page, just me. So it was as a therapy, as a coping mechanism, on how the art is serving the artist.

Christina: *That leads on to the question of whether there have been any moments in your life that have been so difficult that you have abandoned or suppressed your creativity.*

Katarina: When I was a teenager something a bit traumatic happened; now in hindsight it was wonderful, but at the time it was awfully hard. My family moved to another country when I was just beginning my teenage life, just making friends. I was born and raised in Leeds, and we moved to Norway. We had about three months' notice and we just moved, and I had a difficult time in primary school, and I'd just started high school, and there I was so popular and to be taken away from that was incredibly difficult. So art was the solace.

But then, I'll fast forward to my adult life and when I made the decision that art was no longer going to be on the periphery. When you decide that art is going to be your job and to take it seriously, then you start developing complexes that have to do with that.

I came to London to study and started my BA at Wimbledon College of Art, and I began with a bang. It was great, but then something happened through education where I started to feel as if I needed to make money from this somehow. I needed to make work out of something that used to be play, and then it got difficult to initiate the creative process on demand, whereas before it would just come organically, and now I felt like if it wasn't happening, there was something wrong, so I started to develop some anxieties about not doing enough.

Around the second and third year of my BA, I had actually done a lot of work, but I somehow felt like I had done nothing. I thought I couldn't call myself an artist because I hadn't worked all week or month, and I was definitely having imposter syndrome, and I started to feel like not coming up with something often enough was a personal failure. Then of course, you are killing the creativity even more, and I got in a bad cycle where I wasn't making work and I felt bad about not making work, which made it harder to make work and this went on for about a year. It felt painfully long, for somebody whose only way of entertaining themselves is through making. When you can't make, you don't know what you are doing here on the planet.

Christina: *How did you get through that?*

Katarina: I certainly felt that the more self-conscious I was about the problem, the harder it was to recover. If there was ever a moment where I simply forgot that I had this problem of artist's block, immediately something creative would start happening. I had these periods of not making any work and then I'd give up and say: *you know what, screw art, I'm not going to be an artist, I'm just going to give up*, and then when I gave up it started coming back because I wasn't putting that pressure on myself. So unfortunately, I had to go through many emotional troubles with that, and I would say that during my MA I had a proper depression so then you just can't do anything, and it came to this point where I had to go to therapy, I had to get help. When you drive yourself so hard to the point when you get depression, you must give up because you have to start focusing on the very basic things – trying to be a bit healthier, trying to go outside – but what I would hope is that there is a better way of getting back in the creative process than going through a depression.

Christina: *What you have been through sounds difficult and that it went on for quite a while because it started when you were at Wimbledon and then into your MA.*

Katarina: I think it is wonderful being exposed to so much art and so many different practices, but maybe they affected my confidence a little bit. I came to London expecting that I was going to be surrounded by people I could really relate to, but the practices are so diverse that you are not really going to find like-minded people. You are going to find incredibly different types of people, and I found it difficult to relate to other people's practices. I felt a bit alienated.

Christina: *Where did you look for that reassurance?*

Katarina: Most of my reassurance came from my parents. Maybe the best advice I got was from them; most people have to painstakingly explain to their parents why they chose to be artists whereas in my case, they have been the people that most understood. My dad would tell me: *You didn't go to university to become an artist; you are an artist*, and that was very nice to hear but hard to put into practice. And now that I have had a little bit of teaching experience, I see it in my students as well that, my god they come from such rich experiences and all this world needs is for them just to be them, but then they come and they instantly feel like *I need to put another hat on to make my art*. My worst work is made when I try to put the professional hat on; you have to realise that you are already it and just see what you have, because nobody else has that perspective.

Having had to move to a new country at such a young age, I went to an international school for fresh immigrants, nobody spoke English there. I'm actually Serbian. There was nobody who spoke any language I spoke, and I didn't understand a word of Norwegian, but I very quickly made friends from all around the world, and my first friends were from Thailand, and I had a Congolese friend who would show me Congolese music and how to dance. I was incredibly embarrassed about dancing before that so in my worldview, all of these things sort of shifted, shaped my idea of what art is: pop music from Congo, opera that I would watch on YouTube. We didn't have the means to go to the opera but there were lots of wonderful productions on YouTube which really captured my imagination. I would set myself tasks to just watch all the films by one director. Kubrick one month and then a different director another month, so I was very hungry for those sorts of things. I think maybe part of me was a little bit rebellious to the idea that I should just be looking at painting for example, or just be looking at one form of art. I think I was deliberately trying to curate very disparate media, so I was quite a conscious curator from my teenage years upwards, and I would play games like going to the library and picking five random books, closing my eyes and then reading them no matter what they were, games like that to disrupt my centre of attraction. I never stick to one thing. I was influenced by Cindy Sherman, who I discovered later, so when I think about my influences, they are extremely broad.

Christina: *When do you think that you are most creative?*

Katarina: The thing I need most is privacy. Maybe it has to be with being a performer and being very shy, but even with things like drawing, just knowing that I can do whatever without being judged is incredibly important. So it's less in fact about the materials I have but more the knowledge that no one can see me.

Christina: *How do you feel about moving that work into a public space, from a private space?*

Katarina: For me the feeling goes away completely, and it's a very weird thing; afterwards I feel very much inclined to show it. I want somebody to see it, to see what happened to me in that space when I was alone. I remember having a bit of a romance about this when I was a bit younger, having romantic feelings about the working space of an artist. I remember nights when I was completely alone: it's quiet, the lamp is shining on the desk, and I'm drawing and I look up and I realise I have just been drawing like this for hours, and then I think: *Wow, what a special thing this is,* and then I feel almost a bit of sadness that nobody can see that or experience that how lovely that is. And I tried taping myself work-ing, just documenting it because I thought, *It looks so lovely, what's happening?*

Christina: *What's the piece of work that you feel most proud of?*

Katarina: I work very serially, so if we imagine I have several projects, and they have just been infinite, I just keep adding to them, none of them ever finish. So, let's say in one project there is iteration after iteration, and some of those shine out and some of them less so.

If I take as an example my video performances, it's very easy to see when it worked, and I can usually feel it in the far distance during the making. It's a feeling that I have completely gotten rid of myself in a way, I've succeeded in becoming something else for a short period of time and able to escape the burdens of my own worries and thought patterns that I usually have in my daily life.

Art allows me to escape the normal thought patterns I have and inhabit the working space as if I was another artist. I can see in the video when I am really inhabiting the character. I haven't been able to extract a pattern: *What did I do right on that occasion that it worked out so well?* A student of mine recently said a nice com-ment about those videos of me; I was very grateful to her. She said that what struck her is that the performances feel like they are for me. I suppose performance is a place where you feel judged, you are being watched, assessed, but perhaps that's the virtue of doing these things in privacy, and then ultimately you are just doing it for yourself and then later you decide whether to share it.

Christina: *When you are out of the process, what does it look like then? Do you engage with it again once the work's done? Do you have an inner critic?*

Katarina: When I make a work, I think I am very eager to know whether it works, whether it is good or not. I am very eager to find out if I am going to like this result, so I usually can't help myself watching immediately. Sometimes I've let this critic in at a time when it's a bit too early because only when the experiment is really finished, then I think it's fine to bring the critic in but not when it's still under way. The critic is simply a reader or a viewer, so I want to be entertained by the work, I want to be intrigued by the experi-ment and I need to enjoy it as if I were someone else. Entertainment is quite important to me. I think that art should be entertaining.

Christina: *Going forward, how do you see your art developing? You've had this period where you have found it difficult during your MA and now you are doing a PhD and that's another long road. When it's finished, what do you see happening then? What do you hope for your work?*

Katarina: I think one of the reasons I went on to do a PhD is because I did start to believe that this can generate some kind of knowledge, and so right now I want to learn something from my work, and when I am playing different characters, some intuition starts arising about what a person is, so my PhD is about what a person is but through the lens of fictional characters. I would really like to learn something about my own life as a person through my artwork and then after that for art to be some sort of healthy system for generating questions.

Practice is almost like a system that you want to nurture so that you can go and ask it different things, to consult it in different ways, and so I feel like it has already raised so many questions for me about personhood, and I want to continue nurturing it so it can continue being a tool in a way for thinking about these ideas. I want the practice to be able to continue to serve me in figuring out those questions about personhood, and because it's just so different to any other form of knowledge, I feel like I can directly tamper with the fabric of my being by playacting.

In my career, I was hoping to become somewhere between an academic and an artist, to be teaching art because I really enjoy it and it sort of revitalises me. All artists develop these theories of art, and teaching forces me to reconsider these in dialogue with students, which motivates me. I wanted to have this teaching component to my life, and it's turning out to be quite politically difficult to get into that world, but I want to be making for sure.

Christina: *You have talked about some writing and some drawing and some video film – is that the main thrust of your practice?*

Katarina: Yes, but very recently I have started doing some live performance of a sort of theatrical nature like one-woman plays.

Christina: *Does that feel like quite a leap, quite exciting?*

Katarina: It was terrifying.

When it comes to presenting or being in front of people, my main obstacle was my nerves, so I had to work a lot at calming down. If I can just get past the anxiety, then the performance, when I am in it, well, it's kind of enchanting. You have this power over the audience, you can bewitch them. It's very different to film where I feel like I am in a very different private space, just talking to the lens. The pressure of performing live does often mean that I am very invested in the character because I feel there is no way to do this unless I really believe I am this character. It's very transporting because you are so invested in these characters completely filling you up. It was exhilarating to find out that I could do it because for years I thought I couldn't.

Christina: *You have come through some difficult places, but it sounds as if you've come to a better spot at the moment. Given that you are doing a PhD, it's a quite an achievement because often people can feel quite stuck in that process.*

Katarina: I think I am in a better place now. I think I have managed to work a lot on the problem of what I expect from myself. I had some rather unrealistic expectations, but it's my role to produce a good experiment and then see what comes out of these different iterations. I think that has allowed me to be more productive so I don't feel bad about a piece of work. It's very liberating to not have this sort of personal dismay when something doesn't work. It's nice to be rid of that.

Some things still really puzzle me but looking back at some work and reflecting on how I felt at the time: *How did this turn out to be successful? Why did this turn out not to be successful?* and I can talk about it, play in it, but it's still a bit beyond me!

Postscript

Katarina's work does not perhaps offer the audience a typical route to increasing self-understanding of their own creative selves, but her strategy of using performances of fictionalised characters to reflect on who she is can perhaps encourage the viewer to reflect and play with these questions themselves. Katarina's performances seem to be suggesting that this process can broaden and complicate our understanding of who we think we are and raises exciting questions as to what can happen in our creative life when we allow ourselves to play with identities in this way.

In relation to creative writing, the writer and lecturer Celia Hunt says:

When writers consciously use fictional and poetic techniques to tell their story, they suspend the truth telling intentions inherent in the 'autobiographical pact' and this changes the conceptual frame. Now their primary intention is to use memory or self-experience as a trigger for creative writing with an aesthetic product in view. Paradoxically, it is this suspending of intentions associated with the truth of the self that makes fictional autobiography potentially a very powerful tool for exploring 'truths' that lie beneath the surface of conscious self-knowledge; when people relinquish conscious control over their self-representations, they open up the possibility of thinking about and experiencing themselves differently.

(Hunt, 2010, p. 234)

For me, there are parallels between Celia Hunt's theory and the process Katarina uses to make her films and performances in a way that includes the imaginary, the fictitious and the illusory to story the self. Katarina's method enables her to not only produce fascinating pieces of artwork but is also a process from which she gathers strength, in terms of her sense of self, and agency as an artist.

Katarina declares: "If art is a kind of experiment, my job is to set up a good experiment", and this approach to her artistic process has enabled her to maintain some separation between her personal worth and the artworks that she makes. "The results are the results", she says during our talk. In other words, it's not about whether you are making good or bad art – it's about whether you have set up a worthwhile experiment and set aside judgement about the value of what you have done until the experiment is complete. If the inner critic haunts or stalls your process, it is worth trying Katarina's approach.

Creative Task: Fictionalising as a Way of Expanding Our Creativity

Write a story, make a short film, draw a picture or take a photograph about a fictional character that represents your creativity. What does this person look like, dress like, talk like, what do they want to say? What do you learn about your creative self from this exercise?

Bibliography

Hunt, C. (2010). Therapeutic effects of writing fictional autobiography. *Life Writing*, 4(3), 2310244. DOI: 10.1080/14484528.2010.514142. Accessed 22 September 2014

Ranković, K. (2016). Accessed 21 June 2020. https://youtu.be/pmBggcrkTrQ.

CREATIVE INSPIRATION

Looking Back to Move Forward: A Response to Katarina Ranković

Christina Reading

I have been reading Nancy Princenthal's engrossing autobiography of Agnes Martin (Princenthal, 2015). Martin was an American abstract expressionist painter, famous for her pared back line paintings. Princenthal reminds me that: "Martin called her creative source 'inspiration' and she said that the paintings came to her as visions, complete in every detail, and needed only be scaled up before being realised" (p. 7). But whilst these inner visions or moments of inspiration gave her the images to paint, it was the execution of the idea that was paramount to the creation of the work. As Martin says, "But then to actually accurately put it down, is a long, long way from just knowing what you are going to do" (p. 93). Martin thought of inspiration as a gentle spirit: "That which takes us by surprise – moments of happiness – that is inspiration" (p. 93), and she regarded inspiration "as a universal attribute available to all and that if we can get out of the way of our own intellectualism and get in touch with our inner instinct, a bodily process that we need to allow to speak" (p. 94). In other words, whilst an idea can be the spur to your creativity, how you put this into action and into the world also matters. Martin's view of inspiration resonates with me because whilst an idea for a painting often provides my starting point, it is the process of painting that starts a creative conversation between this initial idea and what manifests on the canvas, with the final painting the outcome of this dialogue.

Like Martin, I'd like to think creative inspiration was a kindly capability that was available to all, but delving into history and gathering stories of inspiration by writers and artists as I do in this chapter means that questions arise for me about whether this is something that can be taken for granted. Instead, I find that historically women somehow seem to have too often been denied their inspiration, judged historically within patriarchy as somehow

DOI: 10.4324/9781003286042-5

lacking this capacity or left without the tools or opportunities to get in touch with this inner instinct as Agnes Martin calls upon women to do (De Beauvoir, 1966).

I remember reading Homer's *Iliad* in my teens at school – a monumental tale of how humankind is portrayed as a puppetry of the family of Greek gods that live on Mount Olympus, presided over by Zeus, the supreme Olympian deity and Minister for Destiny. *The Iliad* is a tale in part about creativity on the battlefield, about how displays of superhuman strength, ingenuity and inspiration are bestowed by the gods according to whom they favour. Mere mortals in the tale can appeal to these Olympian Gods only through rituals and sacrifices to be filled with motivation or the power to win the day so that the course of the battle for the legendary city of Troy reflects how the gods decide who to inspire to superhuman feats.

> Achilles' favourite of Zeus leapt up. Athene cast her tassled aegis around his sturdy shoulders; and the great goddess also shed a golden mist around his head and caused his body to emit a blaze of light.
>
> *(Rieu, 1950, p. 342)*

Rereading the tale now, I find it still gripping, but I am less enamoured than my younger self because now I recognise that narrative is mainly about divinely fated and chosen men, human godlike figures such as the warriors Achilles and Hector. For writers like Homer, ancient heroes are all men driven into a state of divine frenzy because they have received the gift of inspiration from the gods. The women in the story are absent or presented as slaves, property that is stolen or fought over. At best, women are coveted for their beauty (Helen of Troy) or craft skills (Briseis) or often as muses (the lesser gods Aphrodite, Artemis, Athene, Demeter) to pray to or inspire men to action but crucially excluded from the possibility of divine inspiration themselves to be warriors or notable writers. So, I think, that's the problem – right from the start, women are denied their creativity because the gods don't favour her for such gifts; she must be content to be a muse, trophy or to serve at best. To be written about, but not the writer. The painted not the painter.

Agnes Martin's view of creative inspiration seems to stand as an aspiration, an appeal to women in the present of the importance of women getting back in touch with this aspect of ourselves. In the conversation with Katarina Ranković, she talks about the educational and social circumstances that inhibited her confidence in her own creative vision and how finding support for this and building confidence, including dealing with her inner critic, was crucial to finding her creative flow, to feeling in touch with her creative inspiration. In part, the message is that without this sense of connection and confidence in their own voice and capacity for what Marcia Baxter Magolda terms 'self-authorship' (Baxter Magolda 2007, p. 69) – that sense of being aware of your own beliefs, feelings and values guiding your actions – acting on inspirational ideas becomes more difficult. Or as De Beauvoir puts it, "in order to be able to write and in order to be able to accomplish something one must first belong to oneself" (De Beauvoir, 1966, p. 156).

Vernon's 1970 edited collection of essays entitled *Creativity* sits in my bookcase at home, and a flick through gives an insight into the diversity of thought and explanation underpinning our contemporary understanding of creative inspiration (Vernon, 1970). Here in Vernon's collection of essays, creative inspiration is variously accounted for as the result of inner unresolved conflict in the unconscious, especially those relating to events in childhood (Freud, 1908), the pinnacle of a process of self-actualisation or reaching full human potential, (Rogers, 1954), lucky genes (Stein & Heinze, 1960), family background and education (Torrance, 1962), personality characteristics (Cropley, 1967), cognitive ability and intelligence (Wallach & Kogan, 1965), a process and related to preparation and skill (Wallas, 1926) or the result of "driving absorption in their work" (Roe, 1952). These texts are presented as objective analysis and evidence on the nature of creative inspiration and the conditions for creative achievement, but the most startling fact is that however accounted for in terms of theories or outcomes, these traits are not associated historically with women. Introducing these texts, Vernon writes: "But an unanswered question is why so few women have shown outstanding creativity in any field" (Vernon, 1970, p. 14). Men are the subject of these investigations with women set aside as a puzzle, reduced to a query about why they seem to be insufficiently inspired to make their mark in the world with their creative endeavours. Of course, I could dismiss these ideas as old hat, not relevant to the contemporary discussion of women's creative inspiration, but it seems to me that it's important to at least acknowledge this backdrop, so that we understand that inspiration hasn't always been associated with women and that reclaiming it and retaining women's right to access it and recognition for its manifestations has a relatedly recent history and is an ongoing endeavour.

In the 1990s, when I was at art college, the article by Linda Nochlin, 'Why Have There Been No Great Women Artists?' (Nochlin, 1971) was a staple of any reading list, a cornerstone of a revisionist feminist art history, which accepted the need to, and efforts made to find and recuperate lost, forgotten and overlooked works by women artists, to challenge and democratise the existing canon. It's fair to say that the article prompted a revision of art history with curators being sent into basements to dig out long forgotten works by women and display them in public spaces prompted by the first big show Women Artists (1550–1950) at the Brooklyn Museum curated by Ann Sutherland Harris and Linda Nochlin (Nochlin, 2020, p. 322). As I write, there is an exhibition on at the Royal Academy called: *Making Modernism* (12 November 2022–12 February 2023) with work by Paula Moderson-Becker,

Kathe Kollwitz, Gabriele Munter and Marianne Werefkin exploring their contribution to modernism. I reflect how attempts to retrieve and recuperate women's art history and assess their creative achievements have the potential to shift our collective assessment of what is to be valued as art, judged to be creative. Looking around the exhibition, their themes of motherhood, portraiture, self-portraiture and their surroundings signal their shared concerns rooted in the personal, the domestic, the familiar. That seems like progress because here is an exhibition of German women artists that acknowledges their contribution to modernism and the changes that occurred in society the late 19th and early 20th century. Women artists who dare to paint self-portraits and family life. But as I look around, I notice that 90% of the audience are women and I wonder what this says. Perhaps that what is valued, what matters to women continues to be overlooked or side-lined or viewed as women's interests. I reflect that there is still work to do to ensure that what matters to women, what inspires her creativity is important to all.

But important as this strategy of retrieval and recuperation for restoring women's creativity has been, as Linda Nochlin says during a conversation with Maura Reilly, "I thought that simply looking into women artists of the past would not really change our estimation of their value" (Nochlin, 2020, p. 20). Therefore, it was also important to consider the constraints of the circumstances in which women were and are making art, the prejudice, the marginalisation and the categorising of women's art and craft that explain why there are no female Michelangelos, why women were judged not to be creatively inspired to produce great art. Nochlin's goal was to explain why women's opportunities to make great art have been restricted through history. As she puts it: "Rather I was interested to see what women had achieved and not achieved within a specific historical circumstances and particular sorts of social refusal and permission" (Nochlin, 2020, p. 19). And so, I decide to look at stories that provide an insight into why women's inspiration seems to be denied to her or is not valued or judged as outstanding in its outcomes, and to look at the ways women can be creatively inspired on their own terms and to find out what conditions support and encourage them to do that.

> On the walls of the gallery, side by side, hangs a long row of heavy, gilt frames, each of them adorned with a coroneted plate of pure gold, on which is engraved the name of a princess: Donna Christina, Donna Ines, Donna Jacintha Lenora, Donna Maria. And each of these frames encloses a square cut from a royal wedding sheet.
>
> *(Dinesen, 1957, pp. 99–105)*

As an art student in London during the late 1990s, I took part in an exhibition in the now fashionable Brick Lane. The exhibition was called *Unmarked*, inspired by an article by Susan Gubar (1981) entitled 'The Blank Page and the

Issues of Female Creativity'. In this article, Gubar recounts Isak Dinesen's short fable, 'The Blank Page', a tale of the blood-stained sheets of royal brides displayed every year by the Carmelite nuns in Portugal for pilgrims and passers-by. And into the faded markings of the canvases, Dinesen tells how

> people of some imagination and sensibility may read all the signs of the zodiac: the Scales, the Scorpion, the Lion, the Twins. Or they may find pictures from their own world of ideas there: a rose, a heart, a sword – or even a heart pierced through with a sword.
>
> *(1957, pp. 99–105)*

So that from these markings viewers looked for omens and made forecasts of the life in store for the royal bride. But ultimately these stained bloody sheets were meant to signal and display the royal bride's purity, her chastity before marriage, the fact that she was before marriage, unmarked. Dinesen writes:

> On the morning after the wedding of a daughter of the house, and before the morning had yet been handed over, the Chamberlain or High Steward from a balcony of the palace would hang out the sheet of the night and would solemnly proclaim: Virginem eam tenemus – *we declare her to have been a virgin* – such a sheet was never afterwards washed or again lain on.
>
> *(Dinesen, 1957, pp. 99–105)*

But read differently, from a feminist perspective as Susan Gubar does, the blood-stained sheets were read of course as a sign of the young bride's oppression, her wounds, and her exchange as object, as currency and trophy within a world of men. In Gubar's revision of Isak Dinesen's original story, the blood-stained sheets are works of art created by the royal brides using the only means at her disposal, her blood. For Gubar it is a women's pain, her wounds and losses that are displayed by those discoloured marks on the canvases.

> if artistic creativity is likened to biological creativity, the terror of inspiration for women is experienced quite literally as the terror of being entered, deflowered, possessed, taken, had, broken, ravished – all words that illustrate the pain of the passive self whose boundaries are being violated.
>
> *(Gubar, 1981, p. 257)*

Gubar makes a broader point, arguing that women artists, like the royal brides, can find that their creativity is inspired by their desire to give visibility and representation to the wounds inflicted upon them by their historic exclusion, and silence within a patriarchal culture. This suggests that finding ways to give representations to these wounds in the symbolic, to find redress and represent women's experiences, means going back into the history of women's collective and personal wounds and making work that stems from those experiences or a reimagining of those experiences. But as Gubar says, these histories of silence, of pain, of blood can be an unsettling and painful place from which to draw inspiration, however powerful and compelling these sources of inspiration may be for women artists and writers. And I reflect that whilst I agree that potentially representing these wounds can be cathartic, because they give visibility in the symbolic to all that has been excluded and silenced from discourse, it nevertheless can take real courage to delve into these wounds and share these vulnerabilities, historical and contemporary with the world.

I remember seeing Tracey Emin's exhibition *The Loneliness of the Soul*, where she used her paintings as the means to express her personal experience of ageing, sexuality and loneliness, in the aftermath of her experience of cancer. Certainly, the rows of emotionally charged paintings seemed to declare the depths of her despair as she tried to come to terms with her experience and the accompanying Instagram of her stoma bag attests to the reality of her post-cancer life. I had never seen a stoma bag before, let alone thought about what it must be like to try and live and love with this piece of medical equipment as a constant companion, but viewing these works I could see and feel the courage it took for her to show this experience. The bravery and generosity of Tracy Emin's exhibition humbles me because I know in the aftermath of my own experiences of cancer, my inclination was to hide away from the world, and for a long while I stopped painting and writing, frozen in an iceberg of fear. And I would not have had the courage to move on from that stuck place, that painful place full of wounds and a sense of loss without the support of my friend and collaborator, Jess, who stepped forward and coached me out of my isolation. Together in our book *Walking for Creative Recovery* (Reading & Moriarty, 2022) we documented, using image and text, our creative recoveries in the aftermath of our own experiences of cancer and showed how walking, talking and reflecting on these experiences helped us to recover our creativity and that doing this in a shared and collaborative way was crucial to our willingness to address the emotional and practical challenges we faced along the way. So, I have found that whilst there was some cathartic power in drawing inspiration from painful memories or experiences, doing this alone would have been difficult and that approaching such challenges in a shared and collaborative way offers a perhaps less terrifying route.

> But in the midst of the long row there hangs a canvas which differs from the others. The frame of it is as fine and as heavy as any, and as proudly as any carries the golden plate with the royal crown. But on this one plate no name is inscribed, and the linen within the frame is snow-white from corner to comer, a blank page.
>
> *(Dinesen, 1957, pp. 99–105)*

In Gubar's retelling of Dinesen's story, she reminds us that the order of Carmelite nuns in Portugal also displayed one sheet that was unmarked. And the tale goes on to say that it was in front of this blank canvas that the pilgrims paused the longest and looked the most thoughtful as they gazed upon its pristine surface. Dinesen writes,

> It is in front of this piece of pure white linen that the old princesses of Portugal – worldly wise, dutiful, long-suffering queens, wives and mothers – and their noble old playmates, bridesmaids and maids-of-honour have most often stood still. It is in front of the blank page that old and young nuns, with the Mother Abbess herself, sink into deepest thought.
>
> *(Dinesen, 1957, pp. 99–105)*

This discussion invites us to speculate on the absence and silence signaled by the blank sheet. Why I wonder, did the absent royal princess fail to comply, not do what was expected of her? Did she run away? Refuse her husband? Was she punished for this act of resistance and defiance? I can only fill the blank page, not with fact, but with my imagination. And in my mind's eye I see this unknown princess astride a horse, galloping off towards a better yet mysterious future, feeling the wind in her hair, joy and freedom in her heart. In reality, of course, this is utopian, a fairy tale, but the image functions as a symbol of women casting off social constraints that limit a woman's potential and the freedom to choose her own path.

The storyteller, in Dinesen's tale, reminds us that it is of the utmost significance that the nuns do not leave out this rogue blank canvas in their displays but remain loyal to the ritual, to the whole story, and allow its silence and blankness to speak. This means that the canvas is not just part of the tale but perhaps even its most potent element because the blankness provides a space for our imagination and creativity to stir. As Gubar puts it, "the blank page contains all stories not no stories, just as silence contains all potential sound and white all colours" (Gubar, 1981, p. 257).

For Gubar, the unmarked sheet represents a space which isn't already stained by the history of a women's invisibility, exclusion, silence within the culture and instead creates the opportunity for women to lay down memories that are not inspired solely by all that she has lost and been denied within patriarchy. She declares that "the blank space, a female inner space represents readiness for inspiration in creation, the self-conceived to dedicate to its own potential divinity" (Gubar, 1981, p. 261). And indeed, it is through the blankness, and silence this canvas offers that a space emerges for women to write stories and make artworks that speak of their potential, of their imagined futures, untethered by histories of loss and the pain of exclusion. To allow different kinds of stories to unfold, stories that come from her power and her own gods. And I like to believe that this book that I write now with Jess, with its stories and conversations of women's creativity, is part of my personal effort to gather and write on the blank space messages inspired by our hope and strength.

These stories of women's creativity are often ignored or not valued by patriarchy but circulate in a different economy outside the dominant paradigm, stories that refer to the reality of women's lives, stories of creativity shared and passed between generations of women, stories from our grandmothers, our mothers, distant aunts. It was through my mother that I learnt about and cherished the stories of my grandmother's seamstress skills, her ability to make clothes for her children and how she passed these interests on to my mother and then, in turn, to my sisters and me. And I have tried to pass these inheritances onto my own children. My children are all adults now, but recently my mother and I travelled to London to spend the day with one of my daughters to make curtains for her new home – a skill being passed down between the generations, a skill that circulates between us.

Stories that maintain a loyalty to what Dinesen refers to as the whole story of women's lives that include the blank and silent spaces in the tale as the Carmelite nuns did through their commitment to displaying of all the canvases, even the unmarked one. In other words, our creativity must deal with these wounds of the past, redress our exclusions to allow women to heal, but we also must imagine that this space can be used to write new histories and look to create positive futures.

The smooth unmarked page is, as Adrienne Rich said: "promise of a time when it can be denied that our power and our pain don't come from the same source" (Rich, 1978 cited in Gubar, 1981, p. 258). This sense of a women's creativity powered by loss and the need for reparation has on occasion been a powerful motivator for many women artists' work including my own work, but it must be admitted that inspiration that comes only from our blood means that it is upon that basis that the story of women's creativity unfolds. Rather the blank sheet is an invitation to women artists and creatives to offer stories stirred by women's resistance and defiance and their liberation so that the story of our inspiration and creativity comes from this place as well.

> Women's creativity, in other words, is prior to literacy, the sisterhood produces the blank sheets needed to accomplish writing.
> *(Gubar, 1981, p. 259)*

In Isak Dinesen's story, Gubar reminds us that the nuns were the weavers of the fine flax linen cloth on which all the royal brides left the faded marks of their virginal blood. Remember, Gubar says, that women are the creators of all that comes first, before those who write, because they make what is written on, they make the cloth. Gubar writes: "no woman is a blank page every woman is the author of the page and the author of the pages author. The art of producing essentials children, food, clothing is women's ultimate creativity" (Gubar, 1981, p. 260). She continues: "the blank page is a tribute to what has been devalued as mere craft or service" (Gubar, 1981, p. 260). In her article, Gubar reflects on the fact that women historically have been the ones that give birth, make the homes, that feed and care for those that become authors, makers, creators. This creativity comes first and is the soil from which all creatives emerge and the help that she provides in her home that allows others to flourish or otherwise is a source of her creativity.

I visit a retrospective of the sculptor Louise Bourgeois (1911–2010) called the *Woven Child* at the Hayward Gallery (9 February–15 May 2022). I have always been interested in her work, especially those pieces that she produced in her 80s during the 1990s that drew on her memories of growing up in her parents' upholstery shop. In her fabric towers (Untitled, 2001) for instance, she uses the tapestry associated with her childhood home. It was her method of using the needle and large, sometimes clumsy, stiches to make her woven cloth sculptures that intrigued me. This was because of the symbolism she provided of the needle (as opposite to the pin) as a tool for repairing and mending things that had been damaged or broken, a process that valued what had historically been rejected as a simple domestic task rather than an artform.

Here Bourgeois has used her personal memories of loss and pain relating to her childhood to inspire, but as the writer Francis Morris has said, "there can be no simple chronology to her art because she lives with her memories, treasures them and at the same time, all the time is traumatised by them: there is no closure" (Morris, 2007, p. 17). It seems to me that Bourgeois offers not a blank page on which to imagine our futures but the message that we can use our creativity to dismantle the old, faded canvases and reconfigure them anew. What she seems to suggest is that the story of our inspiration may not just be about either the spaces marked by our blood or the blank pristine canvas but about taking the marked canvases down from their revered place of the gallery walls and using them to make something anew from the histories of pain and loss that are stained on them. I reflect that women living within the hierarchy of patriarchy have spent their time reimagining what it would be like to live in a world without these structures that marginalise them, so that the ability to imagine another way of living continues to be crucial to addressing these imbalances. And that the ability to consider the question of what women want the world to look like gains more significance and urgency in a world where we need our creativity to inspire us to address the big issues impacting the lives of women across the globe: issues relating to religion, to the environment, to our use of new technology. How do we use our creativity to propel us towards more positive futures which assure our freedoms? For instance, how do we creatively address the fact that engagement with social media platforms can be damaging to our mental health?

Although I sometimes enjoy and benefit from looking at the work and lives of other artists on platforms such as Instagram, I can feel the pull of a sense of self dependent on its instantaneous gratification feedback loops provided by the system of likes and followers. Too few followers, like me, and you feel like a nobody, too many and you are dismissed as a marketing gimmick, but certainly I know that spending too much time in this space can leave me and my creative practice feeling fragmented because my everyday world with its sometimes messier interactions and struggles sometimes fails to compare favourably with the silhouette views of other artists' lives and achievements presented through the lens of social media.

A pause makes me realise I am straying away from my topic of inspiration here, but the discussion does make me ask myself the question, *Why am I making the work that I do?* For me, it's not for fame or money, and it's not always simply because I love what I do – because sometimes it's hard work and unsatisfactory in terms of what is produced – but I reflect that what motivates me is a belief that being creative helps me to get to know myself a little better, improves my sense of 'self-authorship' and shakes off the shackles of restrictive thinking that erodes confidence to move into a space which is freer and kinder to myself and others. Finding ways to support and encourage women's creativity by sharing stories of their experiences is what inspires me. And in the conversation with the performance artist Katarina Ranković, we see how she uses fictionalising, or storytelling, as a way to challenge the notion of a fixed sense of self through a reflective, imaginative process that invites in a sense of openness in terms of who she is as a person and, more importantly, who she might become.

Conclusion

> I knew I had done something important. I wrote it under a kind of heady inspiration that was based on a great deal of previous thinking and knowledge, all of which surfaced as I wrote, each new element led me to further investigation in a wide variety of fields, each discovery demanded further research. I hesitate to use the term "dialectical thinking loosely, but I think of it as such; it was a truly exciting experience. I might tone down the rhetoric a little if I were writing a similar piece today, but somehow at the time, it was necessary to the project.
>
> *(Nochlin, 2020, p. 16)*

The more I hone my creative skills, give time and attention to the practice of writing, to paintings, look at the work of other artists, listen to and read about the ideas of other writers, the more I learn about the questions that motivate me, that spur my creative practice, the more likely I find that inspiration, with its flashes of insight or the flourishes of skills, visits me, and I am able to do something with its gifts. I find that my inspiration can't be forced but engaging with these activities seems to leave me more able to recognise and respond to inspiration when it arrives. Without this effort, this work and learning, I find my inspiration is more elusive, less likely to show up or result in a line of inquiry that impels me or has wings.

And in the conversation with Katarina, what she has to say about her creative practice seems to echo this experience. Inspiration doesn't just arrive, she says – it is the result of setting up a process or an investigation into a subject matter and that for her that subject matter is personhood, aspects of self and her fictional characters are her methods for doing this. In other words, it's the questions that she asks about selfhood that trigger the performances that inspire her and motivate her creative endeavours.

Creative Task: Reclaiming the Past

Reflect on these questions:

- What do you love doing?
- What motivates you to make the creative work that you do?
- What are the reasons that you make the creative work that you do?

I sometimes use old archival photographs or images from art history as inspiration for paintings. A precious family album and its collection of dog-eared prints is a testament of the unfolding story of our family history. The collection seems to fizzle out when my eldest child, Lizzie, is about nine years old, reflecting my move to a less cumbersome way of recording our lives offered via mobile phones. And of course, although I now take so many more photographs, unarguably none are as looked at, as precious as those old prints. So, I use these old prints as a starting point for paintings, transforming them and making something new for the now. Use an old photograph, story, or poem to inspire a new painting or a new story. Reclaim the story, make it your own.

Bibliography

Baxter Magolda, M. B. (2007). Innovative educational practice reveals the secrets to enabling complex learning and self-authorship. Self-authorship: The foundation for twenty-first-century education. In *New directions for teaching and learning*. Wiley Periodicals, Inc. Published online in Wiley InterScience (www.interscience.wiley. com) 109, 69.83. DOI: 10.1002/tl.266

Cropley, A. J. (1967). S-R psychology and cognitive psychology. In P. E. Vernon (Ed.), *Creativity, selected readings* (1970). Penguin Books Ltd.

De Beauvoir, S. (1966). Women and creativity. In M. Simons and M. Timmerman (Eds.), *Feminist writings* (2015). University of Illinois Press, pp. 155–178.

Dinesen, I. (1957). *The blank page*. Last Tales.

Freud, S. (1908). Creative writers and day-dreaming. In P. E. Vernon (Ed.), *Creativity, selected readings* (1970). Penguin Education, Penguin Books Ltd.

Gubar, S. (1981). The blank page and the issue of female creativity. *Writing and Sexual Difference Critical Inquiry, 8*(2), 243–263.

Hayward Gallery South Bank Centre, Louise Bourgeois: The Woven Child (9 February–15 May 2022) Exhibition.

Morris, F. (2007). *Louise bourgeois*. Tate Publishing.

Nochlin, L (1971) *Why have there been no great women artists?, Art news, Jan 1971* in Reilly, M (ed) (2020) *Women Artists, The Linda Nochlin Reader,* Thames and Hudson, London, pp. 42–68.

Nochlin, L (2007) *Women artists Then and Now: Painting, Sculpture, and then Image of Self in Reilly, Global Feminism: New Directions in Contemporary Art 2007* in Reilly M (ed) (2015) *Women Artists, The Linda Nochlin Reader,* Thames and Hudson, London, pp. 322–350.

Nochlin, L A and Reilly, M (2020) A *Dialogue with Linda Nochlin the Maverick She.* Reilly M (ed) (2020) *Women Artists, The Linda Nochlin Reader,* Thames and Hudson, London, pp. 8–41.

Princenthal, N. (2015). *Agnes Martin: Her life and art*. Thames and Hudson.

Reading, C., & Moriarty, J. (2022). *Walking for creative recovery: A handbook for creatives, with insight and ideas for supporting your creative life*. Triarchy Press.

Reilly, M. (Ed.) (2020) *Women artists: The Linda Nochlin reader* (pp. 42–68). Thames and Hudson Ltd.

Reilly, M. (2020). A dialogue with Linda Nochlin, the Maverick She. In M. Reilly (Ed.), *Women artists: The Linda Nochlin reader* (pp. 8–41). Thames and Hudson.

Rieu, E. V. (1950). *Homer: The Iliad, a new translation*. Penguin Classics.

Roe, A. A. (1952). Psychologist examines sixty-four eminent scientists. *Scientific American, 187*.

Rogers, C. (1954). Towards a theory of creativity. In P. E. Vernon (Ed.), *Creativity: Selected readings* (1970). Penguin Books Ltd.

Royal Academy (2021). Tracey Emin/Edvard Munch, The Loneliness of the Soul 7 December 2020–28 February 2021.

Royal Academy (2022). *Making Modernism,* (Paula Moderson-Becker, Kathe Kollwitz, Gabriele Munter and Marianne Werefkin), 12 November 2022–12 February 2023.

Stein, M. I., & Heinze, S. J. (1960). A summary of Galton's hereditary genius. In P. E. Vernon (Ed.), *Creativity: Selected readings* (1970). Penguin Books Ltd.

Torrance, E. P. (1962). Causes for concern. In P. E. Vernon (Ed.), *Creativity: Selected readings* (1970) Penguin Books Ltd.

Vernon, P. E. (1970). *Creativity: Selected readings*. Penguin Books Ltd.

Wallach, M. A., & Kogan, N. (1965). A new look at the creativity-intelligence distinction. In Vernon, P. E., (Ed.) *Creativity: Selected readings* (1970). Penguin Books Ltd.

Wallas, G. (1926). The art of thought. In P. E. Vernon (Ed.), *Creativity: Selected readings* (1970). Penguin Education, Penguin Books Ltd.

3

TAKING CHARGE OF WHAT YOU CAN TAKE CHARGE OF

A Conversation with Sonia Overall

Jess Moriarty

Sonia Overall is an academic from Canterbury Christ Church, where she leads their successful Creative Writing MA. Her work on psychogeography, walking and adopting a researched but sometimes playful approach to creativity has always inspired me, and I have quoted Sonia in pretty much everything I've published on creativity and walking. Her combination of personal and evocative storytelling, always beautifully crafted and deftly researched, helped to change my view that in order to be a published academic, you have to be dry, omnipotent expert (Moriarty, 2014), which, when I tried writing that way, always amplified my inner critic, making me feel like an imposter who didn't belong in HE. Instead, Sonia's work is enjoyable and wise, a rarity in the world of peer-reviewed panels and outputs.

When Chris and I started thinking about people to interview for the book, Sonia's name was top of my list of academics we might speak to. Six weeks into lockdown and relegated to the bedroom whilst my children home-schooled at the dining table (and all over the house) and my husband tried to hold on to his job in the living room, I suddenly wondered if meeting people you truly admire is such a good idea. I had met Sonia before, several years ago at a conference where her talk on walking and responding to place received unanimously positive feedback from delegates from arts and academic backgrounds, but we had spoken only briefly. What if, unlike her writing, Sonia was not humane, wise and fun? I reminded myself that I once met Glenn Close in a toilet, and she is still a hero. Suffice to say Sonia is like her writing, and I felt better as a writer, teacher, person for having spoken to her.

DOI: 10.4324/9781003286042-6

Jess: *What's your earliest memory of being creative?*

Sonia: I remember at a very young age, my mother had one of those very old-fashioned folding bureau desks; it looked like a cupboard, and you could pull out the front and it would become a little desk and I used to say that was my writing space. I would just sit and write probably the worst poetry imaginable, but I used to just write poetry there all the time and there were times when the desk had to be shut because I wouldn't do anything else. But yes, an absolute obsession with books always [laughs], and my parents are really creative, and my father was a musician and he was always off doing gigs and my mother was an artist and a craft maker, so I was kind of surrounded by people making and doing so it wasn't a strange thing. I was the only writer, but we are all readers. It was already there, I think.

Jess: *That's a lovely image of you at the desk. Do you remember how old you were when that started?*

Sonia: Goodness, I don't know. I remember being at nursery school and coming home and already reading and writing and scribbling, probably scribbling nonsense, but scribbling.

Jess: *The scribbling counts, I think. I still scribble.*

Sonia: [laughs]

Jess: *Do you sit at a desk now when you work? Is that where you do your writing? Are there any similarities or none at all?*

Sonia: I think there are similarities in that if I'm really involved in a project, so if I'm writing a book or it's a long work, I will always write longhand and usually in pencil.

Jess: *[Slightly horrified] Really?*

Sonia: Yeah, I write longhand notes all the time. It's kind of planning, longhand planning, and part of my process is to transfer that, to type up, and that's where the editing, the first editing stage happens, and everything gets locked into place; but yeah, I do write with a pencil still.

Jess: *Is that a romantic thing? Is it something about how the ideas translate? Or does it feel different with a pencil?*

Sonia: Yeah, it's just how it comes out. I laugh with my students and say pencil is not the best thing for posterity, obviously you open an old notebook and half of it has gone and faded, and I think it's fear of commitment [laughs]. I think I write in pencil because I expect things to change, and I feel that there is – I'm self-psychologising here – but there is something about the freedom of being allowed to make mistakes The pencil allows you to make mistakes, and that's essential for me. One of my strategies for ignoring the inner critic is that the pencil can always go, it's not permanent, so it gives me a freedom to try things out. I write a lot of notes in very inconvenient places, so I try to carry a notebook with me because I've found ideas come at the least convenient time: when I'm not at the desk.

Jess: *I'm really interested – sorry this is slightly off piste – in that idea of permission to make mistakes and because it feels like in academic work, we're not given that permission. Even though we encourage our students to take risks and not worry about making mistakes, to take a gamble sometimes, it feels that we don't always say that to ourselves as academics. So, is that something about the academic work or is that how you feel in general?*

Sonia: I think that's how I feel in general. I came to my academic practice as a creative practitioner. I was always torn, even at university, about if I wanted to be a writer or if I want to be an academic; the writer was stronger and I think one feeds the other, so I try and carry it over as much as I can.

Jess: *That's really interesting because I think there is something about the austere font on the page that does have that stamp of expecting precise things. I can't read my own writing anymore, but I really love that idea of pencil being more permission giving.*

   You talked about your parents as being both creative people. Did you walk as a family? Were there any things that have inroads into the work you do now?

Sonia: Yes, I was thinking about this a little while ago when somebody asked me, *How does one become a psychogeographer?* My parents used to do this thing – we had to be quite creative about holidays because there wasn't much money, so we had a caravan and we used to load the caravan up, and sometimes my mother would get the map out, we'd get to the end of the road and she'd get the map out, and she'd just go like that [makes gesture] and we'd drive to it and sometimes we'd get to the end of the road and she'd say, *Left or right?* And she'd say, *That's fine, it looks like we're going towards Norfolk!* So fine, let's go to Norfolk! So that's psychogeography [laughs], isn't it? That willingness to just not know where you're going.

Jess: *Yeah, and also letting you make big choices at a young age; that's incredible.*

Sonia: Yeah, that's my parents, very playful and quite silly. That's good, that's useful.

Jess: *Is that something you try to encourage in your students as well?*

Sonia: Oh yeah, absolutely, that playfulness. Planning is essential obviously, you need to be able to know where you're going for a novel, you can't sit down and write a novel and not know where you're going. But the fun part is all of the experimentation that happens first and that allows you to find out where you're going. You might not know until you get there, and then you realise how it's all coming together.

It's tricky, isn't it? It's a balance between being free and playful and experimental – which I really encourage my students to do – and then actually applying a bit of spade work to that and making it fit.

Jess: *I think you're absolutely right; sometimes that playfulness gets muted down especially when students have the pressure of paying for courses as well.*

Sonia: The other thing is that there can be a real preciousness about writing and there doesn't need to be; there really doesn't need to be.

Jess: *I'm skipping on a bit in the questions, you're interested in collaboration and interested in working and experimenting with different forms and different styles. Can you just talk a little bit about that in terms of why that's important to your creative process?*

Sonia: Well, I think it's easy to become a bit navel gazing when you're working on your own. We're always drawing off other people, other influences. When I'm stuck and feel completely out of love with my work, I just have to read something that gives me a good kick and reminds me why I'm doing it in the first place. So that's somebody informing me just through the act of reading. Working with other people is brilliant because it brings a different way of seeing the world.

So, my husband, we've collaborated on other things, he's an artist, a puppet maker and for years we did puppetry together, and I would do the writing and he would have the performance and making aspect. That's brilliant, you're kind of in a similar place, you're bouncing off each other all the time. I've recently done quite a lot of participatory collaboration with a walking textile artist, Elspeth (Billie Penfold), and again she's come from a different cultural place, so a completely different way of seeing art. She's not a writer, but something just happens, and it's exciting when these things come together.

Jess: *A lot of my work is autoethnography, and is accused of being inward facing, but the last book that I did, every chapter was collaborative and I've been working with different artists and people that work with different mediums as well, and like you say, it really kicks me the same way – when you read a particular book, it gives you that spur on. I feel I have a responsibility to them (people I write with) to up my game I suppose too, in a really positive way, not in a pressurised way.*

So, we mentioned the inner critic a little bit earlier, but do you have a strong inner critic, or have you developed tools for skipping past them?

Sonia: Yes, kind of, I think it's really useful, but I do feel that I've tamed it a bit.

I have a tendency to write economically and tight and short anyway, and I think that's taming the critic in that I'm filtering out what

I don't need. But I think the best thing to do with it, apart from giving yourself the permission to say. well, *I don't need you yet, you'll be useful later*, is just distance and space. The number of times I've written something and thought, *Well that's a pile of crap*, then you put it in a drawer and look at it again six months later and go, *Hang on a minute that's all right, that's not that bad.*

You spend too much time with yourself writing [laughs], and that space is essential. And it's also important to satisfy the inner critic a certain amount before you share your work with someone. Beta readers are amazing – I always say to my students we need to be each other's beta readers, but you need to be in a strong enough place first, because if someone walks all over your piece, before you've satisfied yourself with it and know you're ready to take that criticism is crushing and that's not useful.

Jess: *Even after all these years I still find that so difficult to impress on students, and I do get that as well when you've written something and you're riding that wave, but taking that time to leave it in a drawer or something like that and go back to it in a bit is important. Have you got anything that works to help other people to get past critics? Because that's a large part of what this book is about too.*

Sonia: It is giving yourself that space and refusing to look, refusing to re-read, even if it's just for a couple of days. The next day is the most dangerous time, I think. If I'm into something and I've already switched the critic off then I can do it, but if it's a fresh project, I cannot look at what I wrote the day before, because I would just undo it all. Because there is no foothold yet, so my strongest piece of advice would be to leave it at least 24 hours before you look at it again, at least.

Jess: *And do you have people that you know you can go to for feedback and critique, or do you know when you have a sense of when this is working and when this is right?*

Sonia: I think that gets stronger with practice, definitely. I was very uncertain for a long time and after a lull I'm very uncertain, but my husband is my beta reader; he's amazing. When I write a novel, he reads it back to me as I go; I'm very lucky that he'll do that. But he's also very generous, so he's not going to say *that's rubbish*.

Jess: *So, he's a trusted beta reader?*

Sonia: He's a trusted beta reader, yeah.

Jess: *Because my husband works in construction so basically neither one of us knows what the other one does, which we find quite useful. I don't think he's ever read any of my work. He's very supportive, he's home-schooling the children at the moment and is a much more playful home-schooler than I am! But it's a really interesting insight to think about what it's like to live with a person who's a huge part of your process.*

In terms of your thinking process, that idea of the parallels between walking and writing. How has the lockdown affected that? And what are the tools you need to be creative?

Sonia: I need headspace, and I really do need a bit of alone time, and that's very hard to get anyway. With the walking, actually, lockdown's not really stopped me because when I was schlepping in and out of work, and the only walking I was getting was to and from the bus stop, so at the moment I've got more freedom and more time which is strange, so I am walking every day. I'm walking with my son as well, and he's always up for a playful walk, so I've been taking him on some of my manipulated drifts if you like. I also started #DistanceDrift on Twitter. I was contacted by a couple of archaeologists who got copies of my Drift Deck. They were saying about how they might use it to do contained walks over lockdown, and I said we could all do it together, that would be fun. So, I started that on a Sunday morning. It's just me sending walking prompts to people and we've had people all over the place doing this, all over their homes, walking around their gardens, taking longer walks, so it's not stopped me from doing it. If anything, I'm doing more of it because I'm facilitating it for other people as well.

Jess: *So, are there any other things, apart from the headspace and the needing to walk, is there anything else that you rely on in order to get into a heightened creative space?*

Sonia: Consistency of time is always a problem, isn't it? That's the really hard thing; so is carving out a bit of time, even if is only a short amount of time. I've always struggled with finding time in a busy day, but it's essential. If you want to keep going, you've got to do it.

I was always quite bad at that: *Oh no, I can't start that, I haven't got time, I can't start writing that now because I need a full day or I need a whole clear week,* and sometimes I really do, I do need that kind of run up, but once I've had it, then it will sustain me and even if it's ten minutes a day I can just do a bit more and a bit more. Being able to work in a consistent window is the ideal, even if it's like half an hour first thing in the morning. It would be brilliant if I could do that, but it's really quite difficult. That kind of consistent pattern of time is useful.

Jess: *I do find that I need longer periods of time and finding those, like you say, especially if you're juggling all sorts of other commitments, whatever they are, can be really hard. My writing ideally needs a four-hour stretch or eight- hour stretch or but now in lockdown, even 20 minutes can be really difficult. I find I'm walking more though – with my children – but doing the same walk every day!*

Sonia: I quite relish walking the same walk. Some people get frustrated. My husband was saying: *Oh god, it feels like groundhog day, we do the same every day*, but I like that because I like those tiny differences and I do think that no walk is ever the same, ever. I quite like finding those little differences, but that's just the way my brain works.

Jess: *Are there particular things hinder or demotivate your creativity?*

Sonia: Yeah, email [laughs].

Jess: *Oh yes, yes!*

Sonia: My inbox is the worst time eater. I think the world would be so much better without email, I really do. I really resent it and the level of anxiety it creates. I had a couple of weeks off in order to have that run up to some writing, and it was great, I got loads done. And when I had to open my email for the first time after that break, I thought I was going to be physically sick. I was so anxious, because it's like having vertigo, you feel yourself going down this enormous hole of needless communication. I had over 200 emails when I came back from leave. I don't know why people find it so necessary to send an email about nothing! It could be such a great tool if it was used like memos used to be used – people used to write memos because it was an essential piece of communication, not because they wanted to bat something at somebody else needlessly.

Jess: *It's that immediacy. It's like: I've got this thought in my head, I'm going to …*

Sonia: Yeah, that, *I'm going to push that onto someone else to deal with now*, and I know we all do it. I know I do it; I think *I must ask so and so about something*, so I'll send them an email, but of course it's even worse now, that's the worst thing for me, that's the thing that really kills my headspace – hugely, horribly demotivating.

Jess: *I think I am addicted to email. I hate going to bed at night and having messages in my inbox and it is like smoking – even though I'm thinking this is bad for me, I still do it! And often if you're writing the emails are pinging in the corner of your screen.*

Sonia: I always turn it off. I close email if I'm writing. I have to, I can't do anything otherwise. The phone's off, everything's off, because I've discovered that I will write much better if I don't have an internet connection because you know when you get that little thought, *Oh, I'll just check*, you don't have to check it right now; put a line under it, look at it later!

Jess: *That's another really good thing about walking – when I'm walking, I can't be checking my email.*

Sonia: I think it's interesting that when I have an idea, when it's a fresh idea for something or I have one of those *ah-ha* moments where something is solved, it's never when I'm at my computer, it's never when I'm at my desk, it's when I'm going for a walk. Or it's when I'm in the shower or in some kind of contained social situation that doesn't allow me to do anything else.

I always remember that I had a vision of the opening scene of my first novel while I was at a wedding. I was sitting at a table, and I wrote it on the back of a napkin – which I've still got actually, which is quite pleasing. But it's almost as if I needed to be somewhere where I couldn't be doing anything else, where all I could do was talk to the people there. All of the busyness was over. When there is nothing else, it will come. You know, at one point the only ideas I ever seemed to have were in the shower, and we talked about putting a white board in the bathroom so I could just write ideas down. We never did it, but keeping an idea – from the moment you have it to the point of writing it down – can be quite difficult.

Jess: *That's why notebooks can be so useful. Students use phones a lot now too, but it's still all tied up with social media, email and everything else.*

Sonia: You can't just sit there and have a look at the writing and not be distracted by something else. I do say to students, *Please don't use your phones, please write it down*. I don't know if this is changing with the ability to text really fast.

Jess: *Have you got any tips about how you give yourself that headspace now? You mentioned turning off email.*

Sonia: I do take myself off yeah, I take myself for a walk, even if it's just for a three-minute walk yeah.

Jess: *I meant a writing retreat or anything like that.*

Sonia: If only! I have done occasionally. I did have, yeah, I mean it's difficult when you've got family as well, I did have a few days which was an enormous treat just holed up in a chalet, it doesn't sound like a treat, but it was, it was great. Three days where I just got thousands and thousands of words written. That was wonderful, but it's just so hard to do that in a normal everyday situation. You've almost got to re-create the feeling of being on a writing retreat, even if it's for half an hour, pretending the rest of the world doesn't exist, shutting the door, finding a space of your own to write in, which is hard as well. I mean my son is always climbing up here. My study is now at the top of the house, this is an old attic space, but he's always coming up.

Jess: *Yeah, because Paul and I both have work offices, we don't have a study space at home so if we're working from home, we'll work at the kitchen table. But now, of course, there's actually five of us, studying or working at home, so that's why I'm in my bedroom today!*

Is there a specific time you can think of when you've hit a wall?

Sonia: Yeah, I had a run of things going well when I had an agent and a two-book deal, and I was like yeah, I've got here and this is how it's going to be now. Then all of a sudden, that situation changed from the top down because my editor lost his job as part of a merger and everything just changed. That was really gutting and quite hard to get over. I'd written a third book and nobody would touch it, and then I had my son, so suddenly the world was completely different again, and I thought well that's kind of the end of that really, the end of my writing. And I knew it wasn't because I knew I couldn't *not* write, but that was tough and I was very ill when I was pregnant; I got Bell's Palsy, which I've still got residual effect from, so kind of rock bottom stuff. It's a bit like having a stroke really, you can still move, so I started writing poetry again. I hadn't written poetry since I was little and that was the tipping point. I couldn't write another novel, it was too big, too horrible, but five minutes when you're not breastfeeding or something – you don't even get to have a hot cup of tea for about two years! So, I found I was suddenly writing fragments of poetry and that's how I got back into writing and how I started doing psychogeography more seriously. I was constantly out with my son walking; he was strapped to my front or in a pushchair. I think all of those things just got me back into it, in quite a determined way.

Jess: *Especially if you got a tiny child as well, it's really hard to put your health first.*

Sonia: Oh god yeah, it's very difficult. It's also awful because it's the time when everyone wants photos of you, and everyone wants you to be glowing and marvellous, and of course you just feel like shit. But that's a whole other world, the problems of trying to be creative with young children.

Jess: *It's really interesting what you're saying about this idea about fragments. I used to lead writing retreats before I had children, and I haven't been on or run a retreat since I had them. I do think when people say give yourself that 20 minutes or half an hour, I think some people think that's not really meaningful time, but actually you can make that time meaningful, and just saying you're going to go for a three-minute walk rather than a three-hour walk, and what you said about poetry then, because the idea of writing something huge and finished feels so overwhelming when because you've had children or because of your health, but poetry allows you the satisfaction of writing something, of completing something, the feeling you've achieved something or said something. It doesn't have to be reams and reams.*

Sonia: And also writing fragments like that, because my poetry and prose has crossed over a lot means that you're just sowing seeds. The images you've pinned down are there and you can mine them later, they can become something else. I've got so many notebooks full, and what happened is I've become a lot more systematic; I never used to be systematic, I've got box files of early – you know, I was telling you about the napkin thing, I've just got scraps, I just wrote of scraps all the time because I didn't need to structure my time in the way I need to now. I was a lot freer and I could have piles and bits and pieces everywhere, and now I have, especially with full-time work as well, I have notebooks that are indexed, and I know where everything is, it's always with me. I had to become a lot more organised, and I think that helped too, taking charge of what you can take charge of.

Jess: *Yes, can you say a bit more about that? Because I completely agree with what you've been saying about playing, and I've recently written something about wanting to be slightly wilder in my writing and in my practice, because academia, I think, made me quite controlled and not playful. But actually, there is a kind of positive thing about organisation in your approach and creativity as well; could you say a little bit more about that?*

Sonia: Yeah, I'm a firm believer that playfulness needs to happen, but boundaries are useful too, and it goes from the smallest thing like indexing or numbering the pages in your notebook, to deciding that you're going to write a piece that is completely constrained, like a piece of writing where you say, *I'm only going to use words of four syllables, I'm only going use line lengths of eight beats*, anything like that, it kind of allowed, rules can also be permissions, do you know what I mean? There are ways of saying I'm going to work completely differently in these parameters now, and then you can switch those on and off, but yeah being organised, there's nothing worse than writing something and not being able to find it again. It's a horrible feeling, and I haven't got time for it anymore.

Jess: *How do you organise the writing in fragments, do you keep folders or boxes?*

Sonia: Yeah, I've got box files –

> Sonia turns the camera to show her office which – understandably perhaps! – feels like a mix of the cosy, intimate, lived and also professional with boxes and boxes of notes and files.

Jess: *Oh, my goodness, that is a proper collection of box files!*

Sonia: Those are all works in progress. It's a horrible mess, it's a big mess of my stuff that's happening at the moment.

Jess: *Lovely study space though. I've got study space envy!*

Sonia: These are things that have got to the printed-out stage, and there is a manuscript there that I've done nothing with, but I also have lists and notebooks like this that I fill up, so my in-tray has got old notebooks in it. But this kind of approach, it's almost entirely my work, my universe and bloody lists of jobs, endless lists of jobs, it's also a way of – if I have a moment – I can write something, I write it in there and then I can find it again and cross reference it, but I also have big pads that I do longhand and that'll go in the box file, so lots of different ways really.

Jess: *And is it important to you that you're sort of immersed in that?*

Sonia: It's ideal, although I did discover this last week when I was writing, the weather was nice and I took my notes and laptop and sat on a bench at the end of the garden; I couldn't get Wi-Fi and I was really productive. If I'd been here, I would have just been checking, *and thinking, I'll just find that notebook*, so actually that was another form of constraint because in the garden I had nothing in front of me, just my notebook and my laptop, and it worked, it worked really well. I suppose you've got to find different ways, you know?

Jess: *It seems like there is a real balance of play and making time and things like having lists and having your work easily accessible around you as well, a happy balance.*

Sonia: Yeah, and in my office at work – which I can't access at the moment – I started to pull blank sheets from flip charts, because I like working big with ideas sometimes, so I masking-taped a wall of flip charts because I could suddenly leap up with a fat pen and go, *Oh I need to do that* and then it would still be there and I would be next to it and it would go in by osmosis until it was consolidated enough and then I would take it down and then I would remember what that thing was when I wanted to write it.

Jess: *Is that important to you, not constantly, but when it feels right, adjusting your process trying something a bit different?*

Sonia: Well yeah, I do like to mix it up, and I think it's good to find new ways all the time. I've made it sound like my university work kills my creativity, but it doesn't, the volume of work does. Actually, teaching is an amazing way of finding out what works and what doesn't work. I've got students making suggestions, I've got wonderful colleagues. My colleague Peggy Riley works in a very different way to me, she's a great one for saying, *Oh, have you tried this* or making suggestions about how to find space; she's very good at reminding me to find space.

Jess: *I completely agree with you, the volume of work that just kills the creativity in academic work at the moment. It's not some of the people I work with or the amazing students, it just feels like there is this kind of tidal wave of stuff all the time.*

    What's the best advice you've ever had or just an example of good advice?

Sonia: I had good advice from a colleague at work, who is working somewhere else now. He was massively productive and I remember saying to him once: *How on earth do you get so much done?* He was programme director, he was supervising loads of students, but he was making academic work all the time, and he was the person that said to me do something every day, even if it's for two minutes, because part of the problem is the self-loathing that comes with not having done anything and I think that's brilliant advice. Even if you just write a sentence, you've got the monkey off your back, you know that it's possible.

Jess: *It's the dread sometimes that is the worst, so that's really good advice.*

Sonia: Yeah, it's really good advice. Just that thing of find the time, it doesn't matter how much time, even if it's a tiny bit.

Jess: *I know your new book is out next year. Congratulations! People will want a book on pilgrimages next year. That's going to be perfect timing.*

Sonia: I just hope it all goes to plan, ever since the hiatus in my commercial writing career, I never believe it is going to happen until I'm holding it in my hands.

Jess: *Fingers crossed, but that sounds like a book that we're all going to want to read. Where do you hope you'll go next with your creativity? What are your plans? Are there any big shifts or things that you want to continue doing?*

Sonia: Yeah, well I've started writing a play, which is completely new for me. I've done a lot of adaptation for street performance, but I've never written a play before, and I started it last autumn. I pitched my idea to the Marlowe Theatre in Canterbury, and it was one of the ones that was selected for this week of research and development. My god, what an eye opener, I've never done stuff like that before, it was just wonderful because when you write a novel, you're alone with that novel for a very, very long time before somebody reads it and you get any kind of reaction, but working with a director and actors and a raw script was constant back and forth about your work. I was like, *Wow, this is amazing, they are reading it and they are saying stuff about it right now in front of me, and I wrote it yesterday.* That was terrific and I know it's a very different medium and I've got a lot to learn about it, but that's exciting. When I was working for a couple of weeks in the break, I was finishing a textbook and I was writing my first monologue and that was really exciting, so I want to keep going with that. I love the idea of a live interpretation of my writing.

Jess: *That sounds great!*

Sonia: So hopefully something will come of that.

Jess: *And people are going to want some live entertainment soon, I think.*

Sonia: We're going to be really hungry for it.

Jess: *I hope so yes, that's one of the things I have really noticed about this time is first of all about how people are hungry to respond to it [Covid-19 pandemic and lockdown] in a creative way, whoever they are, not just people who have been writing or making for a long time but all sorts of people. And also, home-schooling is reminding us how important creativity in children is as well. Unfortunately, it's kind of been bled out of schools in a lot of ways, and yet during this time you realise just how important it is for kids to make things, express how they feel, think and imagine in some way as well, so yeah, I really hope people do celebrate and support the arts when this is all over.*

Sonia: It's a worrying time. It's a worrying time for those companies that might not get to re-open and the venues that might not get to re-open; that's quite scary, but there has also been the Arts Council fund, and whatever one might think of them, they have been very supportive in getting money out to people who really need it.

Jess: *I actually do feel quite optimistic about that. I really hope that hunger and credence that people have given to creativity does carry over. That's actually the end of my questions, but have you got anything else you wanted to mention or say or anything that struck you while we've been talking?*

Sonia: I suppose it's that I think that everyone who does creative work goes through some form of lack of self-belief. I don't know maybe there are people who don't have that, but it's probably essential, at some point. Some kind of existential crisis is inevitable if you're going to be creative, maybe it happens to people a lot, maybe it only happens once or twice. My experience of being found as a writer, getting a two-book deal and *Oh my god, this is happening, this is what I always wanted* and then that ending quite abruptly could have been pretty disastrous, it could have been crushing, but actually in a lot of ways, I've come out as a different practitioner, as a more robust person, more experimental, collaborative and risk-taking as a writer. I think I always did take risks, but you know we adapt and change and that's a good thing. I know a lot of people have had that kind of experience, that things go well and then things don't go so well, and you learn a lot about yourself when things don't go well, more than when it goes well. Part of being a creative thinker is that you will always find a way, you'll always find another thing to do, another way of doing. There's no point in just climbing one mountain is there, because it's going to get steep at some point, it's better to do something else.

Postscript

Sonia has managed to maintain a sense of play in her practice that is incredibly appealing. Academic life – any professional life – can bleed the creativity out of what we do and eat into the time we know or wish we were spending on creative endeavours. Juggling work and personal pressures with creative space is an ongoing battle that she doesn't confess to have beaten but certainly has strategies for merging her love and the romance of her craft – writing with a pen, permission to make mistakes, walking – with her highly acclaimed teaching and research at Canterbury. Her early memories of being allowed to choose the direction they took on family holidays and being trusted to know the right way has filtered into her work now and even when she has been knocked – the severe illness after pregnancy and the (temporary!) halt in her commercial writing career – she has trusted herself to find a way back and through.

This confidence takes time but by reflecting on our autobiographical threads and the moments we felt lost and how we navigated a way back can help us feel surer of a return in the moments we feel lost. In higher education, autobiographical experiences and memories play an important part in supporting the creative process, and students' understanding and engagement with their discipline is based on their previous knowledge and experience (Biggs, 2003). This can also be applied to creative processes and practices outside of academia. Within existing literature there is extensive debate about whether creativity resides in "the person, a process or an outcome" (Dineen et al., 2005, p. 156), but this book argues it is in all of those things and that valuing the unique experiences we all bring to our creative practice can help our confidence with what we produce and also with how we motivate and shift our creative practice after a significant challenge or change. Csikszentmihalyi (1991, p. 248) argues that a process of effective reflection in creative practice requires both "involvement and detachment", meaning that practitioners must be effectively engaged in the work during the process of generating and making material. This active and involved time must be followed by equally dynamic periods of detachment characterised by extensive reflection in which the critical position and aesthetic qualities of work are considered. This time of objectivity can help us feel less personally attached or enmeshed in our creative work, making us feel less vulnerable and able to develop our craft. Embedding opportunities for reflection on experiences that have motivated – and also frustrated – our creativity is therefore essential.

Bibliography

Biggs, J. (2003). *Teaching for quality learning at university*. Open University Press.

Csikszentmihalyi, M. (1991). *Flow: The psychology of optimal experience*. Harper and Row.

Dineen, R., Samuel, E., & Livesey, K. (2005). The promotion of creativity in learners: Theory and practice, *Art, Design & Communication, 4*(3), 115–173.

Moriarty, J. (2014). *Analytical autoethnodrama: Autobiographed and researched experiences with academic writing*. (Bold Visions in Educational Research). Sense Publishers. https://www.sensepublishers.com/catalogs/bookseries/bold-visions-in-educational-research/analytical-autoethnodrama/

Overall, S. (2016). Walking against the current: Generating creative responses to place. *Journal of Writing in Creative Practice, 8*(1), 11–28.

CREATIVE CONVERSATIONS AS A WAY OF RE-ESTABLISHING ACADEMIC JOY: AN AUTOETHNOGRAPHY

A Response to Sonia Overall

Jess Moriarty

Creativity in higher education (HE) is under attack, and this is at least two-pronged: on the one hand, staff are overworked and demotivated by the pressure to do more for less, which inevitably impacts on how we research and how we teach, and on the other, the current government seems hellbent on undermining the arts and humanities by reducing provision in schools and colleges and questioning the value of a degree in creative subjects. As a lecturer in Creative Writing myself, I see that the effects of this pincer movement have been keenly felt, and I have discussed the threat of burnout in earlier work (Moriarty, 2019). Listening to Sonia confidently locate her creativity in people (her parents, her husband), places (at her desk and via her walking/writing practice) and through her imagination (with an emphasis on play), describing how this informs her teaching and her published work, it is clear that maintaining an international research profile that is driven by personal passions is still possible, and I wonder how I can use Sonia's story to fortify my own arsenal. I think sometimes I forget that what we (staff working in the Arts and Humanities) do still matter, or that the feeling gets lost amongst emails, spreadsheets and templates that dominate time I thought I'd be teaching and researching. But this way of weaving creative/critical processes and doing the work we/she/I love doesn't seem to feel precarious to Sonia or vulnerable, despite the seismic shifts in the HE landscape, where students are valued as customers and academics are seen as customer service staff – tasked with pleasing and keeping students as paying guests in universities/guest houses (Moriarty, 2019). Speaking to Sonia, I am reminded of how studying for a qualification in the Arts and Humanities can support students to develop and sustain a professional career and also contribute to the UK's expansive and expanding creative economy by entertaining, informing, uplifting,

DOI: 10.4324/9781003286042-7

moving and inspiring people. There is a responsibility to protect Arts disciplines in HE, currently under attack from a Tory government seeking to value degrees based on how much graduates earn (Weale, 2019). Creative professionals, much like people working in education, rarely do it because of what they earn. We are driven instead by seeing the work we do as inextricably entwined with our identity, how we feel, think and experience the world. But this goes against a government agenda that wants students to earn enough to pay back the loans they have to take out in order to pay for their education and ambitions to learn.

Sonia's work speaks to global challenges around well-being and environment, building on a history of creative work that has a social purpose and recognises how the arts have, can and do reflect, enhance and provoke the world we live in. Creativity is often motivated by a social purpose, and today, how the arts respond to challenges we face in order to tackle the climate crisis, encourage diversity, support people to live well and connect us whilst valuing our differences is a key driver for much creative work – in HE, in domestic spaces and in the professional/cultural world. In the rest of this chapter, I consider how my creativity can be sustained and motivated and how this can form part of the defence for the arts. The section in italics is a story of finding time and space to be inspired and the writing in normal font offers context as to why carving out time and space – as Sonia has managed to do – is so needed if the Arts and Humanities are to prevail.

June 2022

It is a sweaty Brighton evening and having been at the desk in my daughter's room all day in back-to-back online meetings, I peel myself away from the screen and unfurl. T-Rex arms and uptight shoulders release as I try to metamorphosize from digital academic to Jess in the 3D world. The global pandemic meant an urgent shift from face-to-face to online teaching was essential for universities to endure lockdown and support their students, but for many it exacerbated the stress of working in HE (Bruggeman et al., 2022). I feel as if I have become an academic/robot, part machine and part me – digital and real: the epitome of artificial intelligence(!) Today has been relentless: exam boards, frustrated colleagues, students who are overwhelmed and general bureaucracy and admin that never seem to end, regardless of how many hours I put in. I decide there's no time to change and rush out the door, shouting instructions for dinner at my family.

"Where are you going now?" my daughter asks, waving me off from the doorway.

"A book club, book group, I don't even know," I yell out of the window, speeding into the sunset in a bid to make it on time.

As I drive along, the seafront is buzzing as always with people enjoying the warm Wednesday and celebrating summer with beer and chips. I have lived here since I was eight years old and still love Brighton. Its exuberance and eclectic mix of people and places that acknowledges one size does not fit all. Is it perfect? Not at all – we have one of the biggest drug problems in the UK, it is expensive to live here, and we have had an increase in food banks and poverty that reflects the precarity of a post-Brexit, post – or maybe mid? – Covid world where war in Europe seems imminent and the environment is teetering on a brink that humanity is not yet compelled to drag it back from. Despite being LGBTQIA+ friendly, hate crime still occurs across the city, and none of these problems can be escaped or ignored or denied, but Brighton continues to intoxicate, and as I watch the sun melting high above what remains of the West Pier, I feel grateful for the periods of respite from feeling overwhelmed and anxious that my home frequently provides.

In previous work (Moriarty, 2019), I argued that neoliberalism was dismantling higher HE and as part of that, myself very much included, some lecturers were breaking too. The significant increase in administration and pastoral duties – already immense pre-Covid and certainly heightened during lockdown and now, in the aftermath – has disrupted the emphasis on teaching and research, changing the role of the academic and undermining academic freedom. Cuts to funding across HE, but most specifically in the Arts and Humanities, have raised existing barriers to research in these disciplines – and yet academics are still under immense pressure to seem relevant in terms of the Research Excellence Framework (REF) and the Teaching Excellence Framework (TEF) (which measure the impact of an individual academic's work and allocate kudos and funding to the university to which they are affiliated on the basis of this assessment) and produce research that is deemed as having impact by a government hell-bent on cuts and developing a Higher Education Academy (HEA) that is motivated by wealth creation rather than student and staff well-being and academic integrity. The Higher Education Funding Councils (HEFCE) have been managed by the state since it replaced the UK University Grants Committee in 1992, and the effects of this change have spread gradually and insidiously throughout HE. Academics have silently complied with pressure to do a lot, lot more for a lot, lot less, and in the meantime, funding has become all but dried up. A study by the Higher Education Policy Institute identified that the introduction of fees had turned universities into "anxiety machines" (Weale, 2019), whereby the numbers of students and staff being referred for counselling or to occupational health made it clear that there is a crisis in HE "where staff struggle with excessive workloads, precarious contracts and a culture of workplace surveillance" (Weale, 2019). A report from the Education Support Partnership found that 40% of academics are thinking of leaving HE because they are stressed, anxious and disillusioned by the fear of rejection, heavy workloads and administrative pressures (Fazackerly, 2019). This backdrop combined with the aftermath of having skin cancer in 2016 that had resulted in heightened anxiety (luckily the only side effect to date) meant that my motivation for working and researching diminished. I felt a pressure to publish and a pressing need to remind myself that there is still a utopian purpose to teaching HE, one that values learning and people and creativity, and I hoped that the book would satisfy both of these drivers. I felt professionally and personally compelled to write about my autoethnographic experiences of working in HE and to try to find strategies to hold myself together (Hayler, 2017) and address the work:life imbalance that I'd created.

> Another joy of autoethnography thus comes forth: the ability for a person to use writing or performance to navigate pain, work through confusion, express anger, and come to terms with uncertainty. To use writing and performing as therapeutic processes that can help a person better understand, reframe, or work through an experience.
>
> *(Adams, 2012, p. 184)*

And as I excuse myself past tourists and people leaving work, and the day after *Roe v Wade* (Regan, 1979) has been overturned in the US, I am not sure that the world, let alone HE, is holding. There have been seismic shifts affecting how we teach and research, an erosion of our academic freedom (Docherty, 2012), that means the landscape is not always recognisable, the terrain is ragged and rough, and I'm still not sure of my footing. The neoliberal agenda now driving HE is threatening how we work via "a quiet ruination and decay of academic freedom" (Docherty, 2012, p. 47). But despite this turn, academics still join the profession with the optimistic ideal that we are contributing to a better world, or at least better conversations. We don't join for the money or the glory; we join because we have an idea that teaching can make the world a better place (Priyadharshini & Robinson-Pant, 2003; Kelchtermans, 2005; Troman & Raggl, 2008; Marsh, 2015). I didn't join HE because I thought I would be putting emails and meetings and spreadsheets ahead of learning and research, but that is now the part I often play. Ball (2016) argues that it is time to change the conversation, and that instead of despairing for where education is going, we need to either change, or refuse our part in neoliberalism. Via a series of conversations with my co-authors in *Autoethnographies from the Neoliberal Academy*, we identified a series of strategies to help us with that change. They included:

- a resistance to traditional academic writing;
- valuing of personal storytelling and imaginative texts in academic research;

- a space for the writers and readers to reflect on their experience of HE and the effects of neoliberalism on how they teach, research, think;
- creative research methods using dialogue, stories, reflection;
- practical ideas for a more motivated academic practice that requires time off campus, collaborative work, dialogue and reflection, making (image/text).

(Moriarty, 2019)

The collaborative autoethnographic writing, out of which the chapters emerged, brought me into dialogue with my collaborators, who helped me to confront the neoliberal I had (have?) become, whilst considering the academic I want to be, and guiding me on how to move towards that stranger, that other self. These two entities are still not resolved, three years after the book was published, but I feel like the dialogues and writings provided me with a map and directions that have guided my work since then:

My neoliberal self is:	My rewilded self is:
Hard-working	Hard-working
Always stressed	Motivated
Unboundaried	Knows when to stop
Reads emails at 11 pm	Sleeps or has sex at 11 pm
A ghost to my children/students/ colleagues	Present
Always at a desk	Often at a desk, but also works outside, off campus
Tearful	Remembers to smile
Worried	Walks
Isolated	Collaborates
At risk	Vulnerable but aware
Ill	Well
Does work she feels she should	Does work she must
Intimidating	Collegiate
Has no time for students	Makes time for students
Does a lot of work to an OK level	Does focused, doable work very well
Isn't sure she wants to be an academic	Feels she belongs in HE
Is overwhelmed	Is challenged and inspired
Doesn't know what she is if she isn't an academic	Has ideas for what she might do next
Can't be seen in her writing	Values personal and evocative stories (Moriarty, 2019)

Since completing the book, all my autoethnographic work has been in dialogue – collaborative (Chang et al., 2013) – which helps me to resist the critique often thrown at autoethnography, that it is narcissistic navel gazing

(Coffey, 1999), and supports my writing as a method of inquiry (Richardson & St Pierre, 2000). I write and I find out. I discover myself and my collaborator and the social world understudy a little differently, usually a little better. I believe that this is what autoethnography can help us to do and why it is a methodology that can support personal well-being, stimulate creativity and generate rigorous research and pedagogy that whilst academically rigorous, is also personal and evocative (Ellis, 1997). This way of working has, for me, humanised HE, helping me to learn with and from others and employ what Pelias describes as a methodology of the heart (Pelias, 1999). Deleuze and Guattari's concept of 'nomadic' space is useful in regards to my experience of collaborative autoethnography. In *A Thousand Plateaus* (2014), they describe two different kinds of spaces: the striated and the smooth. Striated space can be thought of as bound by measurements and structures that relate more to the methods and protocols of university space, for example. Smooth spaces, on the other hand, are like the seas and deserts of the nomad and are therefore fluid, immeasurable and unpredictable. This kind of space can be thought of in relation to non-traditional academic approaches that value the emotional, the personal and creative (McInally & Moriarty, 2022).

Lorde (1984) makes the case for creative writing (prose and poetry) being valued in academic contexts, in order for people to feel seen and heard whilst maintaining academic rigour. And autoethnography is a methodology that values and encourages – not just writing, but also performing (Spry, 2011), art (Minge, 2007; Reading & Moriarty, 2022), music (Bartleet & Ellis, 2009), poetry (Pelias, 2011) and adaptation (Marr & Moriarty, 2021). And these works are often linked to personal events and challenges including (but not only) eating disorders (Tillmann, 2009), depression (Jago, 2011), child abuse (Ronai, 1996), rape (Minge, 2007) and HIV (Blinne, 2011). But the process of collaborative autoethnography is, for me, pleasurable, offering space outside and away from the neoliberal academy and putting me in touch (or reconnecting me with) a community of peers and friends that supported me to feel better able to navigate the culture in HE that had previously hindered my motivation and purpose. In this way, rather than capturing experiences with pain and trauma, autoethnography becomes a method of support for readers and writers of such texts, that can story experiences of connection, communication and joy. In this way, autoethnography functions as "equipment for living" (Burke, 1974), offering audiences "alternatives for living" (Spry, 2011, p. 12). "A good autoethnography helps make life better" (Adams, 2012, p. 191).

I park in a side street and navigate tourists and people leaving work, on my way to Afrori Books, the first Black bookshop in Brighton that celebrates Black writers and promotes diversity in publishing. The shop is in the North Laines, and as I enter, I spot students and colleagues milling about the space, clutching Misfits *by Michaela Coel (2021), and discussing the book. Mild panic grows in my chest: I thought this was just the launch? I haven't purchased, much less read the book.*

I scan the bookshelves for a copy and my eyes alight on a whole host of books that I want. The bookseller helps me identify and find new authors that my kids might like and wraps all these new treats up for me. I will the summer holidays on so I can lie in the shade and consume them at leisure, no deadlines or feedback needed, just reading for the joy and interest. Feeling restored, I join the group gathering on the sofas and confess that I haven't read the book. Instead, I sit back and listen as people who read their invite in full discuss Coel's novel, talking about institutionalised racism and authorship, making space for one another and personal, lived responses to the writing. Drawing on their lives as archive to share and grow understanding in the room. As I listen, ideas start to buzz and fizz, stimulated by these dynamic dialogues and the stories that are shared – Michaela Coel's writing motivating new knowledge and awareness. This, I realise, is how I make sense of the world. As the exchange extends, I plan a pilot project linking pedagogy and research with community engagement and reflect on my community of practice to identify potential collaborators. I want to stay and find out more, to learn more, but a glance at my watch tells me I am already late. "Thank you so much everyone; that was completely inspiring and uplifting!" I blurt out, gathering keys and books as I race out of this dynamic and joyful space and metamorphose again, this time back into a mum who is late to collect her daughter from football practice and doesn't know what's for tea.

> What emotions do we conjure when we write autoethnography? Although there are certainly exceptions, the majority of evocative autoethnography relies on experiences of hardship, sadness, and pain. Sometimes the pain is something that is overcome, but sadness and anger are usually at the root of those essays.
>
> *(Myers, 2012, p. 158)*

Creative Conversation as a Method of Re-establishing Academic Joy

Autoethnography leans towards capturing challenging lived experiences via storytelling that Ellis (2009) described as being part of the "trauma culture" (p. 372), but this trope in the methodology is potentially problematic for (at least) three reasons:

1 We are in danger of trapping ourselves in narratives of pain that, if published, are in the public realm for good (Moriarty, 2019);
2 We are obliged to story intimate others (Ellis, 2007) in our autoethnographic work, and ethically, this is problematic but especially when the work we are sharing relates to trauma and pain;
3 We are at risk of excluding autoethnographic stories that aren't about pain, which undermines autoethnography's desire to be democratic and inclusive (Moriarty, 2019).

Autoethnographers are looking to use their writing/practice to transform, heal psychological wounds and promote change (Tamas, 2011), but this process need not always be linked to trauma. After all, we learn from experiences of happiness and joy (Myers, 2012) too, and this is not less valuable than the knowledge we derive from experiences of pain. As the culture in HE continues to put pressure on academics, writing about experiences that establish – or re-establish – academic joy has the potential to offer strategies for colleagues struggling in their roles that can make academic life more pleasurable and motivated, thereby resisting a culture of doing more for less that is causing more and more academics to rethink their careers and leave the profession (Fazackerly, 2019). For me, creative conversations about our subjects and disciplines that offer insights into our lived experiences are part of that joy. Hearing the stories of colleagues, students and community partners informs my own pedagogy (Kalume & Moriarty, 2022; Parks, Moriarty, & Vincent, 2022), enhances my creative practice (Reading & Moriarty, 2022; McInally & Moriarty, 2022; Marr & Moriarty, 2021), evolves my research (Parks & Moriarty, 2022) and also nourishes. Speaking to Christina reminds me of how a creative space with time to talk, reflect, think and share stories isn't a luxury or frivolous; instead, it is a part of the creative play or reverie (Reading & Moriarty, 2022) that is a crucial part of our creative process and also supports our well-being. Chris was inspired in earlier work by the notion that:

> Time spent collecting one's thoughts, time to work undisturbed. This is space for contemplation and reverie. It enhances our capacity to create.
> *(bell hooks, 1995 cited in Robinson 2001: 635)*

And as bell hooks (1995) reminds us, finding creative time and space is made more complex, given that many women feel "utterly *overextended*" already by the effort of making money and looking after family. So, the time and space for discussion and contemplation that Christina offers and we then co-create is valuable and important to me.

> I'm thinking here of the wanderings of reverie where the present and past co-exist, where reflection offers up poignancy and understanding that might otherwise be buried.
> *(Talbot, 2017, p. 199)*

The artist and writer Emma Talbot refers to as an "inward movement towards the self" and the opportunity to get to know the "irrational mechanics of our inner lives … the stories of our thoughts and feelings, our dreams, hopes, fears and love" (Talbot 2017, p. 199). And this matters. As autoethnographers, we should not feel compelled to share only stories of pain. Finding moments of joy that sustain our well-being and inform our creative/critical practice offers a way for autoethnography to draw in and include stories that might otherwise be lost, stories of pleasure, hope, happiness.

Creative Task

In the brilliant *Misfits*, Michaela Coel uses a moth to show her relationship with the world and with herself; initially hating and wanting to destroy the moth, she begins to discover a respect and love for these extraordinary creatures, who have been much maligned and wronged, and develops empathy and kindness for them. Think of an animal that you have had an ambivalent relationship with and write about it and you in a way that acknowledges understanding. In lockdown, I became irrationally scared of birds, and so here I choose to story myself as an owl, synonymous with teachers and educators and also under threat.

Strix

Barred Owls live in mature forests,
Nest in hemlock and maple trees,
Sleep in hidden snags.
This species can commonly be found
At home by 8 pm,
Favours cool river corridors,
Open terrain where they can't be
Penned in.
Its plumage is dullish in colour –
Dirty white, mid-brown feathers,
Rusty ruffs that tend to moult at a young age.
Its skull is the size of a medium fist,
Black tipped talons and a needle beak
For killing small mammals, little lizards,
The occasional frog.
This bird has very few offspring,
Is highly territorial, hunts alone.
Like most birds of prey, the female is larger than the male,
Wingspan of up to 35 cms,
Travels 6 miles a day.

On the nearby coast,
They are considered invasive,
Expanding territory and
Taking up space
That was never meant for them.

Bibliography

Adams, T. E. (2012). Possibilities for communication research. In Myers, W. B. (Ed.), *Introduction to writing autoethnographic Joy: Qualitative communication research* (pp. 157–162), 1.2.

Ball, S. (2016). Subjectivity as a site of struggle: Refusing neoliberalism? *British Journal of Sociology of Education, 37*(8), 1129–1146.

Bartleet, B. L., & Ellis, C. (Eds.). (2009). *Music autoethnographies: Making autoethnography sing/making music personal.* Australian Academic Press.

Blinne, K. C. (2011). "I rained": On loving and (un)becoming. *Journal of Loss and Trauma, 16,* 243–257.

Bruggeman, B., Garone, A., Struyven, K., Pynoo, B., & Tondeur, J. (2022). Exploring university teachers' online education during COVID-19: Tensions between enthusiasm and stress. *Computers and Education Open, 3,* 100095.

Burke, K. (1974). *The philosophy of literary form (Vol. 266).* University of California Press.

Chang, H., Ngunjiri, F. W., & Hernandez, K. C. (2013). *Collaborative autoethnography.* Left Coast Press.

Coel, M. (2021). *Misfits: A personal manifesto.* Henry Holt & Co.

Coffey, A. (1999). *The ethnographic self: Fieldwork and representation of identity.* Sage.

Deleuze, G., & Guattari, F. (2014). *A thousand plateaus.* Bloomsbury.

Docherty, T. (2012). Research by numbers. *Index on Censorship, 41*(3).

Ellis, C. (1997). Evocative autoethnography: Writing emotionally about our lives. In W. Tierney, & Y. Lincoln (Eds.), *Representation and the text: Re-framing the narrative voice* (pp. 116–139). State University of New York.

Ellis, C. (2007). Telling secrets, revealing lives: Relational ethics in research with intimate others. *Qualitative Inquiry, 13,* 3–29.

Ellis, C. (2009). *Revision: Autoethnographic reflections on life and work.* Left Coast Press, Inc.

Fazackerly, A. (2019). It's cut-throat': Half of UK academics stressed and 40% thinking of leaving. *The Guardian,* 21 May. www.theguardian.com/education/2019/may/21/cut-throat-half-academics-stressed-thinking-leaving. Accessed 25 May 2019.

Hayler, M. (2017). Thirty two ways to tell a story of teaching: Self-narrative and pedagogy. In M. Hayler, & J. Moriarty (Eds.), *Self-narrative and pedagogy: Stories of experience within teaching and learning* (pp. 1–13). Springer. Studies in Professional Life and Work.

hooks, b. (1995). Art on my Mind: Visual Politics (The New Press, pp. 125–132 in (ed Hilary Robinson 2001) *Feminism-Art Theory. An Anthology* 1968-2000), Blackwell Publishers Ltd. (pp. 635–640).

hooks, b. (1999). *Remembered rapture: The writer at work.* Henry Holt.

Jago, B. J. (2011). Shacking up: An autoethnographic tale of cohabitation. *Qualitative Inquiry, 17,* 204–219.

Kalume, T., & Moriarty, J. (2022). "It's a collaborative affair": Case studies of innovative practice in and across HE. In *The Bloomsbury Handbook of Collaboration in Higher Education: Tales from the Frontline Bloomsbury.*

Kelchtermans, G. (2005). Teachers' emotions in educational reforms: Self-understanding, vulnerable commitment and micropolitical literacy. *Teaching and Teacher Education, 21,* 995–1006.

Lorde, A. (1984). *Sister outsider.* The Crossing Press.

Marr, V., & Moriarty, J. (2021). Reclaiming stories: Invoking the goddess. *Gramarye Journal,* (20). http://www.sussexfolktalecentre.org/journal/

Marsh, S. (2015). Five top reasons people become teachers – and why they quit. *The Guardian,* 27 January.

McInally, F., & Moriarty, J. (2022). Monsters & campfires: Using storytelling to humanise institutional spaces. In J. Moriarty, & K. Aughterson (Eds.), *Performance and wellbeing (performance and communities).* Intellect Books.

Minge, J. M. (2007). The stained body: A fusion of embodied art on rape and love. *Journal of Contemporary Ethnography, 36,* 252–280.

Moriarty, J. (2019). *Autoethnographies from the neoliberal academy: Rewilding, writing and resistance in higher education.* Routledge.

Moriarty, J., & Reading, C. (2019). Supporting our inner compass: An autoethnographic cartography. In J. Moriarty (Ed.), *Autoethnographies from the neoliberal academy: Rewilding, writing and resistance in higher education* (1st ed.). Routledge.

Myers, B. W. (Ed.) (2012) Introduction to writing autoethnographic joy. *Qualitative Communication Research, 1*(2), 157–162.

Parks, M., & Moriarty, J. (2022). Storying autobiographical experiences with gender-based violence: A collaborative autoethnography. *Journal of Autoethnography, 3*(2), 129–143. https://doi.org/10.1525/joae.2022.3.2.129

Parks, M., Moriarty, J., & Vincent, H. (2022). The immobilities of gender-based violence in lockdown: Devising workshops to support women who experienced gender-based violence during the Covid-19 pandemic to tell and share their stories. *LIRIC: The Lapidus International Research and Innovation Community Journal, 2*(2).

Pelias, R. J. (1999). *Writing performance: Poeticizing the researcher's body.* Southern Illinois UP.

Pelias, R. J. (2011). *Leaning: A poetics of personal relations.* Left Coast Press, Inc.

Priyadharshini, E., & Robinson-Pant, A. (2003). The attractions of teaching: An investigation into why people change careers to teach. *Journal of Education for Teaching, 29*(2), 95–112.

Reading, C., & Moriarty, J. (2022). *Walking for creative recovery: A handbook for creatives with insights and ideas for supporting your creative life.* Triarchy Press.

Regan, D. H. (1979). Rewriting Roe v Wade. *Michigan Law Review, 77*(7), 1569–1646.

Richardson, L., & St Pierre, E. (2000). A method of inquiry. *Handbook of qualitative research* (pp. 923–948).

Ronai, C. R. (1996). My mother is mentally retarded. In C. Ellis, & A. P. Bochner (Eds.), *Composing ethnography: Alternative forms of qualitative writing* (pp. 109–131). AltaMira Press.

Spry, T. (2011). *Body, paper, stage: Writing and performing autoethnography.* Left Coast Press, Inc.

Talbot, E., (2017) Overstepping the boundaries: Notes on intimacy. *Journal of Visual Art Practice, 16*(3), 195–212.

Tamas, S. (2011). *Life after leaving: The remains of spousal abuse*. Left Coast Press, Inc.

Tillmann, L. M. (2009). Body and bulimia revisited: Reflections on "a secret life". *Journal of Applied Communication Research, 37*, 98–112.

Troman, G., & Raggl, A. (2008). Primary teacher commitment and the attractions of teaching. *Pedagogy, Culture & Society, 16*(1), 85–99.

Weale, S. (2019). Higher education staff suffer 'epidemic' of poor mental health. *The Guardian*, 23 May. www.theguardian.com/education/2019/may/23/higher-education-staff-suffer-epidemic-of-poor-mental-health. Accessed 1 June 2019.

4

DESIRING A FULFILLED CREATIVE LIFE

A Conversation with Irene Marot

Christina Reading

The chapter includes a reflection on how myth and memory can be used to support the creative process. In her work *The Age* (2022) the artist Emma Talbot has refashioned an out-of-date tale, by transforming the elderly women who appears in Gustave Klimt's painting (*The Three Ages of Women*, 1909) into a wise woman who labours – according to the principles of permaculture – to address the problems of the world. In doing so, Talbot is creating a new myth for a new age, and the reader is asked to engage in a dialogue around their own motivations and how these can be best supported.

I arrive at Irene's house ten minutes early. She hates early. I know that *early doesn't work for her.*

"Didn't you get my text?" she yells across the parking space outside her house. I have arrived at a bad time; she's just heading off in the car to drop her son Daniel, a handsome twenty- something-year-old at the train station. I later find out he has been staying overnight looking after Irene's dog Bosco, a large elderly, rambunctious chocolate Labrador. I have encroached on her last few precious moments with him, stepped into her private zone. She lashes out, defending her territory, her time, and I shrivel back inside my shell, retreating from the tentacles of her displeasure. Almost in the same breath her grip relaxes, and she relents.

"Let yourself in, there's a newspaper on the table. I'll be back soon," she shouts and speeds off in the car, presumably to the station.

I first heard Irene before I saw her, hooting with laughter at a Steiner school summer camp – an event I had gate-crashed in an attempt to inject a bit of creativity and outdoor fun into my son's staid state school education in the mid-90s. Irene was committed to the alternative path for Daniel, whereas I was toe dipping, cherry picking what I perceived to be the good bits from

DOI: 10.4324/9781003286042-8

FIGURE 4.1   Bosco and Sam. Irene Marot. Oil on Canvas.

this experience. I was instantly attracted to Irene's gift for enjoying herself, for living life on her terms, throwing herself wholeheartedly into any situation with joy and able to talk in great depth and with understanding about the vagaries of life and art.

I got to know Irene as a fellow artist and a painter, and only later discovered that her profession as an actress was already established, and that she was well-known for playing DD Dixon in Brookside in the 1990s. I was reminded of this side to her life when I had a birthday party at my house and a cousin from Liverpool yelled excitedly: "It's the lady from Brookside!" reminding me that she was quite a celebrity in a world I had only a peripheral view of. But it is as a painter that I relate to her. I am attracted by the body of work she has developed narrating her family life, painting images of her partner Sam, her son Daniel, her dog Bosco (see Figures 4.1 and 4.2) and the bulls in the field at the end of her garden.

Irene arrives back 20 minutes later, all smiles, her demeanor softer; she has done what she needed to do and is back to her hospitable self. She makes us both an elaborate frothy coffee and offers me a biscuit, a peace offering. She is self-aware enough to know that she can be fierce, but I enjoy this side of her too. Conversation with her is always honest, kind and direct.

Irene potters, not quite ready to settle for the interview. Setting the scene, she lights the wood burning stove, bringing comfort and warmth to the room we are sitting in on a dull and rainy December day. She's animated, keen to tell me about a radio play she has just finished where she played death. "I fucking loved it; I loved it. I was so at home, I was so at home playing death with a sense of humor," she says. "Not only did I love the character," she enthuses, "I didn't have to learn the words so there wasn't any of that problem. I didn't have to look great." She elaborates:

> "It's not so much about me and my visual presence on stage, although I am very comfortable with an audience; it's the words in the mouth and where they have come from of course, the mechanism of it coming from the body. I like the tool. Do you see what I mean?"
>
> The words come up and they come out and you find an intonation so everything you say has to carry the subtlety of the meaning of the word, I love that challenge.

There is a fire in her as she speaks, the aftermath of the play still ebbing through her.

She sits down on the sofa, a signal that she is ready to start the interview. Irene prompts me to test the voice recorder. "So that you don't get to the end and all is lost," Irene warns. Wise words.

Christina: *What are your earliest memories of being creative?*

Irene: It was mostly outside, being outside and creating games outside. It wasn't small and intimate being in the house. We had a couple of planks nailed into the branches of the oak tree in the field end of the garden, and I lived in that tree. I came home from school and climbed up; that tree was the world to me. I've got photos of my brother and sister and me; we used to camp in that field too.

Christina: *Quite outdoorsy then?*

Irene: Yes, totally everything was outside. I remember creating whole worlds outside. I have only one memory of creating anything inside – I organised shows for my parents, endlessly patient grandmother and poor unsuspecting aunty and uncle, and a friend, and I wrote a play about a naughty elf, which we performed in the local church hall, announcing it at school assembly and charging an entrance fee.

Christina: *Games/role plays?*

Irene: Games, lots of games outside with my sister and my brother when he let me into his gang, with my friends. My dad was very playful, strangely enough. He would create competitive games when we went to the beach such as who could jump the furthest down the dunes and he would dig large holes and bury us to our shoulders. He was also very tempestuous, and if he lost his temper, you would duck.

Christina: Where was this?

Irene: On the Wirral. My mum got left a bit of money, and we moved into this big old Victorian house. Next to the house was a tennis court and a field that belonged to them, and my mum very cleverly rented this field. It wasn't very big this field, not as big as our garden, but we did everything in there. We camped with all my friends.

Christina: It sounds quite social.

Irene: Yes, very social, and when we were very little, we lived on an estate that had just started to be built and there were lots of green fields, and every Friday night my dad would create a game for all the kids in our neighbourhood. We would have a game of cricket every Friday night.

Christina: He sounds like he was a bit of a leader then?

Irene: My dad set up the games for everybody; my mum did all the food for everybody. She was a bit of a nurturer. She was a force of nature. She had three kids, ran the Cubs and took in foster children. My mum trained as a nurse during the war, and when we were older – she worked as a midwife on nights, had elderly women board at our house and then opened an acclaimed nursery school. She was never happier than when she had a project in sight. She had all the time in the world for young children and the elderly. Not so patient with the rest of society! And even in her 80s she was still concocting adventures – never afraid to speak her mind.

Christina: Neither of them were actors, were they?

Irene: Oh god, no. Well, my mum could have been, and my dad was a handsome, tall French man with a French accent, and women used to love him. I don't know if he was aware of that.

Christina: He was from Mauritius, wasn't he?

Irene: Yes, their first language is French. So, when he joined the RAF with his tennis racket and dinner jacket and found himself the gunner at the back of a bloody plane, he was posted to Scotland with hardly any English. He didn't know if he was coming or going. I think it was quite a hard time for him, so he was quite an unusual man, my dad. Who he was, I never knew. My brother used to joke that he didn't believe he came from Mauritius and he was putting an accent on, even when we went to Mauritius and met some of my dad's 13 brothers and sisters.

Christina: A bit of an enigma?

Irene: Totally. I used to watch him playing with Daniel, and he would make up the strangest of games, like he would set up ladders next to the fence and they would creep up the ladders and see who was coming and pretend to shoot them and then drop down out of view. Daniel still believes to this day that the marks on his legs were shrapnel wounds.

Christina: *What effect did he have on you, upon your decision to take up acting?*

Irene: None really. My mother, on the other hand, was more of a performer. Quite queenly was my mother. She was also an extremely attractive woman. My sister takes after her, very queenly.

Christina: *Do you think you are more like your dad then?*

Irene: My brother and I are remarkably similar or were before he died. Yes, I think so, more like my dad, and we met all these cousins a couple of years ago in Mauritius who'd also traveled from various parts of the world, and they are all quite feisty and sociable and quite playful people.

Christina: *That's very much like you, isn't it? You sound like you are a microcosm of the community you come from.*

Irene: Yes, and without knowing them. It was nice to spend time with them. My dad was quite gregarious when he was out, in between weeping. He was a very emotional man, but he was happy – he would never have moved from his shed if he didn't have to.

Christina: *But you still feel like you didn't really know him?*

Irene: No, and he got Parkinson's towards the end of his life; most gunners did seemingly.

Christina: *So, as you moved through your education, when were your first stirrings of interest in exploring your creativity?*

Irene: Art, I did art; I was quite gifted at art at school.

Christina: *So, it was there right from the start?*

Irene: Yes, but I can't remember drawing at home strangely enough. I don't remember anybody ever talking to me about it at school. I was an avid reader though. I used to read under the covers in bed, under my desk, anywhere I could get away with finishing a story.

Christina: *What sort of things did you read?*

Irene: Banal fairy stories to begin with. Sue, my sister, and I had a long walk to school, and I used to tell her stories. I was always creating stories about little holes in the wall where the elves lived, the little people. I was quite engaged in that world for quite a long time. Because my sister was younger than me, I could engage in it longer. She loved it, loved it.

Christina: *How old were you when you used to do that?*

Irene: I know it was from 7 to 11 because that is when we moved and had that long walk (to school). My sister and I used to watch the tennis club and pretend that there were strange goings on, and we used to put hats on and take turns in watching. And there were lots of games of being detectives and solving mysteries.

Christina: *Quite performative then?*

Irene:	Yes.
Christina:	*Were there any fairy tales that you remember?*
Irene:	No, nothing comes into my head straightaway. I'll start making it up if I start looking for it. All of them. That world of little people of elves and fairies. And magic – I couldn't get enough of it.
Christina:	*Does that still have resonance now?*
Irene:	Seemingly, because lots of little people live in my garden. Little people, other worlds. I don't know how much of this is about escapism and creating a life that is not mundane. An inner yearning always.
Christina:	*A yearning for what?*
Irene:	I don't know, that's the thing, that's the mystery, the pursuit, the yearning.
Christina:	*Do you mean that you are in touch with your desire?*
Irene:	Yes. It's not as strong as it used to be. The impulse goes. Then without that, what is the point?
Christina:	*Have you had times in your life when it's disappeared?*
Irene:	It is to do with painting, not with acting. With acting, you work within an itinerary. You have a play to put on, you must find your way into a character, and because the inner psyche is eternally exciting, then I would never not want to explore a character. Do you see what I mean?
Christina:	*Never lost it with acting then?*
Irene:	No, but the work is not always available, and even less as you get older and being a woman – so there is always a hunger, but it comes and goes with the painting and that's why it's more of a tumultuous journey for me because I panic slightly when it goes.
Christina:	*Describe that feeling when it goes.*
Irene:	It feels quite empty, a bit of an abyss and there are concerns of *will it ever come back*? So, for me it was quite profound, because I hadn't painted for a long time before the exhibition we did. The Brighton Art Fair is neither here nor there for me but it was more about the fact that I had to sit down and do some painting. I suddenly felt a connection to something, felt an impulse to make these paintings, very exciting, even though the outcome is neither here nor there, I have to say. It was the fact that I felt driven to do these paintings because of the art fair. I had to work on a different scale, which prompted a seemingly different route. So, in the art world it seems like if I don't have a deadline, I can't keep the momentum.
Christina:	*You described how you were gifted at school. Did you abandon that to go into acting? Did you set it aside? How did you make those choices?*

Irene:	Right, yes. I was planning to go to art school in my sixth form. I was doing A Level Art and French, and I was looking at Manchester and Liverpool art school. I didn't think about getting down to London because that was off my radar, as a girl from the Wirral. This circumstance changed my trajectory. My French teacher decided I couldn't do French. My sister also received this hatred from this French teacher, Miss Jones. I didn't have her until sixth form; I had another teacher up until GCSE. Miss Jones hated the both of us.
Christina:	*Why do you think that was?*
	I don't know. She might have hated my sister because she was a beauty. I was never a beauty. I was attractive, blah, blah blah. I have no idea and she never even gave us the reason why I was not allowed to do French. She stopped teaching me, and I never pursued it, which is odd in retrospect and so in retaliation I went, *Fuck you, I'm not staying at school then.* And the thing that kept me the happiest at school was games, I was captain of tennis, I was captain of everything.
Christina:	*Sporty then?*
Irene:	I was so sporty, so sporty. I loved team games, I absolutely loved team games. They tried to encourage me to stay at school because the games teacher wanted to make me head of games and I said: *No, no, fuck this, I'm going.* I was 17, because I did the first year of lower sixth and left then.
Christina:	*It was quite a big decision?*
Irene:	Huge, huge really. I don't remember my parents having any resistance to it. So, the French teacher prompted this different line, of course. So, suddenly I wasn't at school, and I did my A Level at the local art school, and in that year of not being at school I suddenly saw other possibilities.
Christina:	*Do you think you had a sense that you wanted to shift away from that school before the incident with the teacher?*
Irene:	I would have stayed. I was in a play in the lower sixth form with the boys from the boys' school and that was everything and I was hailed, you know what I mean, I played the main character, not the protégée, it was a kind of classic play – *Our Town* by Thornton Wilder, and I fucking loved it. Absolutely loved it. I would never have thought of drama; I did elocution, and I went to ballet with a friend of mine. I wasn't very good at ballet, too restrictive (though I later studied Laban Dance at college), but I was really good at elocution and even though I had a strong Liverpudlian accent, I could interpret poems and prose.
Christina:	*What about written words? My sense is that you might write well.*

Irene:	I didn't particularly think that at all until the guy that marked my MA said it was an interesting piece of work and I could go on with that subject to pursue a PhD, but I am not inclined to write particularly.

I have written a film though. I was doing an adaptation – I always must do something. If I am not inclined to paint, I will always pursue something, whether that's ceramics, pottery, or sculpture, to bring me back to something where I feel desire. Yes, I think the desire is important to me, I think the desire is important to creativity. |
Christina:	*So, what you are describing is a process where if the desire is not in painting, it shifts to another form of expression until you feel it again?*
Irene:	Yes, absolutely, and I will look for it even though I don't know what it is. I'll put feelers out.
Christina:	*Have you had a time when your creativity nosedived and took second place? Or has it always been there?*
Irene:	Most probably after I had Daniel, I probably didn't do anything then. Except I was working at Brookside, so I had that life going on for me. Having Daniel is the most creative thing I've ever done. After I had Daniel, I looked for an art class.
Christina:	*How old were you then?*
Irene:	Fucking 43. I did do a bit of drawing along the way; I've always liked to draw, so I have bits and pieces at home.
Christina:	*So, motherhood brought out a slightly different aspect to your creativity?*
Irene:	Yes, I was still at Brookside, so I was acting but my whole being couldn't wait to get to the painting class. It was only once a week; Dan must have been two or three, my mum would have looked after him while I went for an afternoon. I just got extremely excited.
Christina:	*You describe how even if you don't feel like painting, you go off and do something else. Are there any other things that you might do to keep that language going in your head? That stirring or feeling? But without making?*
Irene:	I think that is when I would pursue, in the past, spirituality. When I was lost, I looked for somebody to do a reading, and that sounds naff and minimal but he (the person that did the reading) was considered quite high up in a tribe of North American Indians, and I started to work with him. That's when I did my night on the mountain of fear, where you stay up all night in the dark on your own in a chosen but unfamiliar space outside and greet your fears and anything else that might arrive and make rituals. Also, with a

FIGURE 4.2   Top Banana. Irene Marot. Oil on Canvas.

friend, I worked with a shaman from South America, so I went to look for a creative energy that wasn't about expression but an internal working, a movement inside which gives you wonder and remembering the magic of our existence.

Christina: *So, when you think of your overall sense of creativity, is it quite a chaotic thing for you or is it quite purposeful?*

Irene: I think chaotic has more resonance. I don't do a lot of sequential thinking, remember, so it will be lateral across things, it will be that way of looking at things rather than purposeful. But there it is. I am always looking – *what is the meaning of life,* you know?

Christina: *You are adventurous, Irene – brave in your pursuit of things.*

Irene: I have been but perhaps less so now. And when I felt a bit trapped this summer, I took myself off to Bath to a Sufi meeting. There was the purposeful going off travelling on my own to discover what Sufism was about.

Christina: *What is Sufism?*

Irene: The truth. The inner truth. It's about peeling away the layers really; something that's attached to nature is always very attractive to me.

Christina: *Does that relate to your early experiences growing up? That sense of being in nature.*

Irene: Yes, I think so, it's about being outside – I think you have it, as well – a yearning to be in nature. It's quite interesting because I don't express that in my painting though.

Christina: *From what I know of your paintings, they always seem to be related to your family, there is always Daniel or Sam or Bosco.*

Irene: It's the dog, mainly. The bloke who ran Art at Brighton said that – which I thought was insightful of him – unless I have connected on a heart level with my subject, it won't happen for me. And I think he is right. So, a friend who was in our studio – he's quite famous now, quite successful – when I used to go in and say, *Oh what am I going to paint*, he said, *It doesn't matter, just have a mess around and something happens* and I take that on board. But it's so not interesting to me, roaming around like that, although I know it can be very productive possibly in the end.

Christina: *It's the notion that if you are an artist, you can just go and sit in an empty place and push things around and come up with some- thing. I know artists that do that, but I know for myself, I hear what you are saying, I need to go into the studio with a sense of pur- pose, with things to do. I can't sit inside in the studio all day.*

Irene: It almost kills me, that.

Christina: *Is there a sense of what you are not doing, or should be doing – a sense of failure perhaps that you are not doing it right?*

Irene: Yes, there is all that side of it as well. It's interesting, and this isn't condescending to other artists, but when a fellow artist asked me which of my paintings sold, I said one of Bosco and Daniel which I haven't really been interested to sell, which I didn't think would sell. I only put it in the exhibition because it was small and fitted the space and she said, *Just do another one*, and I looked at her: *no, it doesn't work like that for me*. It's beyond my comprehen- sion. Once it's done, I have no wish to make that painting again.

Christina: *So, you need to be in that moment?*

Irene: Yes, I think so. When I was at art college and I did a painting all in blue with a white dog going into this wood, well a tutor loved that because it was quite poetic for him, so he said, *Why not do it all in red?* and I hadn't thought of that, and I did it all in red and it was a very different painting. A great exercise. So, I am interested in the exercise of things as well. I thought it was really fascinating to do it like that. I don't know if my heart was in it or not, but both paintings went (sold).

Christina: *So, you talk about your creative process being different in your acting and in your painting. In your painting, you quite like the challenge of an exercise. For instance, the most recent paintings you have done were an exercise and that seemed to give you some discipline. Is that right?*

Irene:	Yes, and also when I have a commission to do, and it's somebody I know, and I am only doing it as a challenge to find my way back into art because I have to think about painting again. Until something strikes me, I don't sit around thinking about painting at all. Whereas I will watch TV and think about the acting and how they are working, and I'll have an opinion about it, but perhaps it's more accessible.
Christina:	*Do you think then that acting is your first love?*
Irene:	I think it is, most probably because it's easier, though I may be trite saying that. I think I'm referring to the joy/dynamics/complexity of working with others. Sharing the responsibility of creating a piece, the process from rehearsal to performance. Telling a story. The energetic fields that one is engaged with in the narratives of a drama is nevertheless exhilarating. The fear the terror, the challenge of being present, not anticipating outcomes. I think with painting it is harder for me to create that line of communication. But you know yourself, the relationship with a painting – being brave enough to stay present and allow the painting what it needs, that singular experience can be lonely and excruciating with odd glimpses of joy.
Christina:	*Your paintings seem to me to be quite sensitive and gentle?*
Irene:	It's most probably the other aspect of me. And maybe it's not always comfortable for me to go there. I don't know.
Christina:	*How would you describe your process in your acting?*
Irene:	So, there is a given process, you'll read and the character will just jump off the page or not. You know it in your psyche, you have part of that person within you already, and then if you don't know it – then you research, then you read the play to see what everybody says about your character and then you read it again to see what your character says about other people, so you are building a picture of that person, and then you see what actions the character takes. Then see what that character speaks and what the character is actually meaning, so the subtext is there, so there is quite a rich tapestry and detective work that you go through.
Chris:	*Is that process comforting in some way to you?*
Irene:	I just find it fascinating. My first job after drama school was with Common Stock; it was a cooperative and they do really interesting work, and we had to devise a play around women, and we went to visit a women's refuge to meet the women.
	It was a play about women survivors. Cherry Potter was writing it and we would improvise all day long around themes, subjects, situations, and she would either record it or take notes and then she went away and wrote the play. During that time – it was probably a six-month period, that's a lot of time, isn't it, to turn yourself

inside out being creative. I find improvisation excruciating. It's not about filling the silence. It's about being absolutely in the moment and being true to the moment. Some people absolutely adore improvisation. I am quite good at it I have to say, but that's more painful than working on a script for me because you can free rein. I think that now we are talking, I've realised I most probably do need some boundaries. I am probably happier with a few boundaries because it releases me somewhere.

Christina: *Is that what the exercise in painting does? It creates a boundary.*

Irene: Yes. That's why I quite enjoyed the botanic painting class I did recently because I had to find a way of working with watercolour, working with a line, working on the paper. Otherwise, I just seem to spread out, spread out and disappear.

Christina: *If you look back at your painting or acting life is there anything you are really proud of?*

Irene: There is a piece of work, a film I made about me and my son, and we are breaking into a house and we are going to squat and we change that house and our lives as we live there. It was on at the National. It was just a lovely time.

Christina: *When did you do that?*

Irene: In my mid-30s most probably, pre-Sam, 36.

Christina: *That's quite homely in a way?*

Irene: It's about creating a place to be and the relationship with the kid. They searched everywhere to find a kid that didn't look like they had been to a kids' drama school. That was a really special time. I was dealing with a slightly broken heart. I don't remember if I had been left at the time. I dreamt that he was going to leave me, that's the weirdest thing and so to come back from Nicaragua where he was making a film and throw myself into this lovely creative place with a warm, supportive cast and crew – the director loved me and I was a bit in love with the cameraman. And we were improvising the script and we were given a lot of freedom with the brief. It just worked. I could be true to me and to it.

Christina: *That seems to me to resonate in everything you do; you can't do anything unless you are true to it.*

Irene: That makes me feel like I am going to weep now, just hearing you say that, and there is a painting that I painted that I wish I had never sold – it's a huge painting, it's like five-to-six feet of a duck's head, it's a duck's head but I think the complexity of that is – I had a hysterectomy which meant I couldn't have another child. And what I did straight afterwards was went out and got six ducks and the ducks in my life are very much about that.

Christina: *A sense of loss?*

Irene:	Yes. So, this big duck's head which would mean nothing to anybody else; I think it just works because it was so mad but filled with loss, regret and gratitude to the ducks.
Chritina:	*But it also came from a place of honesty?*
Irene:	Yes, yes, and these ducks, these funny ducks, these naughty Indian runners that replaced the kid I didn't have as well. It's a great painting, I think it's a great painting.
Christina:	*Just to finish Irene, is there anything else you'd like to say?*
Irene:	I did a tapping workshop (EFT – emotional freedom technique) on creativity and the women who ran it, I rather liked her, she said, *When you get to the studio, do you feel like you ever want to go to sleep?* I said immediately, *Yes, always either sleep or I want to eat.* I remember Irene (a friend who died) used to come to the studio and have something to eat and the same with me. I'll have a sandwich and sit down, and she said that the labour of creativity is like giving birth. I did so much weeping in that workshop, I cannot tell you. While you tap significant parts of your body, you repeat for example, I am talented, courageous, creative, and whatever, I love and accept myself. So, you don't injure yourself having any of these talents or you don't dismiss them. It's hard work. It needs time, it needs to gestate.
Christina:	*Absolutely and you can't just do it out of nowhere.*
Irene:	I have these girlfriends who say to me: *You are such a talented painter; why don't you just go and paint every day?* It makes me feel very angry when they say it.
Christina:	*How do you deal with other people, your critical audience?*
Irene:	There is something for me that is tied up with my own psyche; when I see my completed painting on the wall and even if I think it's not bad, I can hardly look at it. *It's just not good enough* is a real common thing for me. A real common thing. And I avoid the audience. I never make myself present. At the studio, at a PV (private view), I am always found working on the bar.

A friend and I were doing a life drawing class, and we had to talk about our work for five minutes or so. We both nearly had breakdowns. Talking about my work, the pain of it is – somebody once said to me that underneath it somewhere I am quite a shy person and that's where that shyness presents itself – to reveal that very inner core.

It's such an inner place. I remember I hit my head after Irene's (friend) funeral, and I went to see a chiropractor and he said, *What do you do?* and I said, *I am a painter and an actress* and he said to me that acting is on the outside and painting is on the inside. Painting: that is the inner journey.

Postscript

Irene keeps her heart, mind, and eyes open, always. And conversation with her is always honest and direct. All these traits make her exceedingly good company but here she shows us how they also serve her creativity, keeping her motivated, curious and in touch with her own evolving interests.

Her approach to her creative life invites the reader into a consideration of what it is that motivates us to make art and reminds us that sustaining this desire to be creative is not something to be taken for granted; but needs to be nurtured, encouraged and sustained. And the implication is that to do this requires a remapping of the way we view our lives that places creativity at the heart of our decision making and of finding the courage to make the changes to our lives so that we can give our creativity what it needs, what it deserves. I have always found Irene's talent and commitment to her creative process impressive. She treats it seriously and with care, taking the time to tune into what it wants and what she needs to sustain it, whether that means changing the medium she works in, learning a new creative skill, a walk in the country-side or a trip away to renew her spiritual sense of self. But the commitment to a creative life doesn't always lead to economic security or fame, as Irene acknowledges, because amid the dreams and ambitions for our creativity, she readily acknowledges that compromise often provides a backdrop, the terrain on which our options are reconfigured. Despite this, Irene's message is that the choice to follow a creative path brings its own riches in terms of a life led that always embraces new horizons.

CREATIVITY, MYTH, AND MEMORY

A Response to Irene Marot

Christina Reading

Emma Talbot's exhibition, *The Age*, for which she won the Max Mara Women's Art prize, opened at London's Whitechapel in 2022. I make the trip to London to look at her work, excited because of the way that she combines imaginative storytelling, personal experience and eco-feminism in her artwork, and these themes are also intrinsic to my own practice.

In the gallery there is an installation that consists of a sequence of floor-to-ceiling painted silk panels, surrounded by knitted sculptures and animations. The exhibition begins with the elderly women who feature in Gustave Klimt's painting, *The Three Ages of Women* (1909). Talbot uses her installation to transform the depiction of Klimt's older woman from a woman shamed by her age, her lack of fertility, her redundancy in a world of men, to a heroine – a wise and wild woman who is the protagonist of a new story more reflective of our age. A woman who rails against the problems caused by capitalism, patriarchy, ecological disaster, rapid technological innovation and sprawling urbanization that have left the earth scorched and polluted (Talbot & von Stauffenberg, 2022, pp. 65–80).

I am interested because Talbot's installation takes classical Greek mythology as its starting point, namely, the 12 labors of Hercules attributed to the poem written by Peisander in about 600 BC, but reworks it to place the old woman from the Klimt painting at the centre of the story. In the original tale, Hercules – nearing the end of his life – is transformed into a god by completing a series of trials as an act of penitence in the service of King Eurystheus. Composed as a continuous narrative, each of these trials requires Hercules to use violence and theft in order to complete them. In Talbot's retelling of this ancient tale, she considers what methods the old woman would have used if presented with similar challenges but within a contemporary context to

DOI: 10.4324/9781003286042-9

address current problems. Talbot said of this work, "I imagined that if an elderly woman thought about how to reorder the way we live to survive for the future, she would also have to go to the roots of power structures and change them" (Talbot & Stauffenberg, 2022, p. 67). And so rather than employing the Herculean approach, Talbot depicts the older woman adopting the 12 design principles of permaculture to guide her actions. I learn from the exhibition that permaculture is a way of living that integrates land, people, resources and the environment in ways that are mutually beneficial to all. The design principles are scrawled in ink across the silk panels:

1 observe and interact
2 catch and store energy
3 obtain a yield
4 apply self-regulation and accept feedback
5 use and value renewable resources and services
6 produce no waste
7 design from patterns to details
8 integrate rather than segregate
9 use small slow solutions
10 use and value diversity
11 use edges and value the marginal
12 creatively use and respond to change

(Smith, L. & Fray-Smith, W. (2022) p. 36-7)

Talbot's wise woman uses these principles to guide her efforts and resolve the problems facing the world in a way that is in tune with the rhythms of nature and kinder and fairer for all. Earth care, people care and fair share are at the heart of her message and the message of permaculture.

This brings me back to my conversation with Irene because I felt that in the telling of her personal fable, Irene too is a wise woman, walking her own path, suggesting a creativity that nourishes and sustains us, embraces nature and accounts for the needs of others. Her message is that the creative life is also a journey, a struggle sometimes, its trials, ups and downs due to the vagaries of fate and the consequences of the decisions we make of our own free will, but that wherever that chain of events and choices leads us, Irene urges us to follow her own design principles:

1 take responsibility for shaping a creative life in which you look after yourself
2 make sure your lifestyle supports that journey
3 have a place to work
4 have friends and family to support you
5 make time for activities that spark the imagination

6 remain open and receptive to things beyond your immediate understanding
7 leave room for the magical, the unbelievable, the spiritual (if that's relevant to you)

Of course, she acknowledges that women historically have faced difficulty and hostility creating the conditions favourable to support creative ambitions, but we are urged to take that trip, sign up for that course, have a day off, do what it takes to nurture your creativity.

As Irene asserts, artists/writers need clear goals that sustain the desire to pursue creative ambitions. Talbot says about her approach to artmaking,

> "I only make work about what I'm really preoccupied by or interested in at the time, so my work reflects my own thoughts and experiences as well as issues that are part of a wider contemporary context. I know when I feel really motivated and believe in ideas. If I don't feel really connected to something, I can't make work about it.
> *(Talbot, E., & Von Stauffenberg, B. (2022). p. 73)*

What motivates differs of course between individuals, but this wish to be creative is not, as Irene reminds us, something to be taken for granted, and it may require different creative outlets during a lifetime to ensure the motivation is sustained.

In his book *Missing Out* (2012), Adam Philips argues: "we have to resist our wanting being stolen from us before we realise it", because it is our wanting, the pursuit of our desires that makes life worth living (Philips, 2012, p. i). As Irene says so succinctly in the interview, without this, "What is the point?" I think perhaps that Irene's story cannot be understood fully without understanding her pursuit of a personal truth, however intangible that might be to others: a reminder that telling our story is always a subjective endeavour that speaks not just of the objective events and circumstances of our life but also signals what matters to us, what we value. As Jung has pointed out, "the only question is whether what I tell is my own fable, my own truth" (Jung, 2019, p. 13). Once when I was stuck for inspiration about what to paint, Irene simply said, 'paint what is in your heart' and I have found that to be such a useful guide in my own creative journey to check I am pursuing the things that matter to me. The story Irene tells of her creative life is ultimately a story of what she has appreciated on her journey. Irene instinctively knows that trying new things, being open to new experiences, can play a key role in helping to keep motivation and interest in our own creativity alive (Beaty et al., 2016). Irene's own creative path has sometimes been audacious, involving dramatic shifts in her direction of travel, but like the wise women in Talbot's installation, Irene is always the heroine of her own story, and she survives all to tell her tale. Currently, it seems to me that her paintings that focus on her domestic life reflect the fact that she has reached a haven of sorts, surrounded by her partner Sam, her son Daniel, her family and friends and her dog Bosco.

And my conversation with Irene also reminds me that the act of telling the story of your creative life or storying the journey of your life is also first and foremost an act of recollection, prompted by the questions I ask. What unfolds is a chronology of the things that she remembers as being most potent to her story at the time of our conversation. This makes me think about the part that memories play in the stories we tell about our lives, and I return to Plato's ancient texts to see what has been said:

> For what is in the word recollection but the departure of knowledge, which is ever being forgotten, and is renewed and preserved by recollection, and appears to be the same although in reality new, according to the law by which all mortal things are preserved not absolutely the same, but my substitution, the old wornout morality leaving behind another new and similar existence – unlike the divine, which is eternally and wholly the same.
>
> *(Plato, 201c–212a in Sesonske, 1965, p. 42)*

For Plato, man has a desire to be immortal, and the only way this can be achieved is through constant reinvention of the Self, in which each aspect of the Self, our feelings, thoughts emotions, bodies, even our souls, is involved in an endless process of casting off the old and the remaking of Self anew. Plato does not view the Self as a fixed, static or permanent thing, but rather involved in a constant process of evolution and change. Significantly here, Plato extends this argument to our memories, suggesting that the act of remembering means substituting the original memory with a new one that we have summoned up through our recollection (Plato, 201c–212a, in Sesonske, 1965). As memories change, so must the part they play in our evolving sense of Self.

In Plato's dialogue between Socrates and Agathon, Socrates recounts his conversation with Diotima of Mantinea to Agathon, a woman like Talbot's protagonist, "wise in the many other kinds of knowledge" (Plato, 201c–212a, in Sesonske, 1965, p. 38).

> Marvel not she said … if you believe that love is of the immortal, as we have several times acknowledged; for her again on the same principle, the mortal nature is seeking as far as possible to be everlasting and immortal: and this is only attained by generation, because generation always leaves behind a new and different existence in the place of the old.
>
> *(Plato, 201c–212a, in Sesonske, 1965, p. 42)*

The way I make sense of this ancient idea is to think of each act of recollection as part of a process of representing the original memory, so that the old is replaced by the new/current version, and that each new memory builds on the last version that we have stored away in our minds/bodies – like an archive of self. The same each time, but also different.

When Plato wrote these words, rigid patriarchal traditions of the time would have meant that stories of women's lives were lost, and today we can largely only speculate on what women's experiences were like at the time. But like Talbot, I think these ancient ideas can be looked at again, and that the artist can revisit an imaginary past, placing women's experience at the heart of the enterprise.

I am interested that Jess, like other contemporary women writers, has recently ventured back into the distant past, reimagining and rewriting these ancient mythical tales to include the perspectives and voices of women overlooked at the time: for instance, Pat Barker's *The Women of Troy* (2021) and *The Silence of the Girls* (2018); Madeline Miller, *Circe* (2018), and *The Song of Achilles* (2011); and Vanessa Marr (2021) evokes Demeter in *Reclaiming Stories, Invoking the Goddess*. All have used the overlooked past rather than relying on the gods to inspire their creative work in the present. The experience of these unknown women still matters to present-day women writers, and they draw upon an archaeological imagination rather than gathering facts to bring these ancient stories into the present. They reclaim their past to belong to themselves more fully in the present.

The point of remembering or re-remembering or even reimagining women's experience is not some narcissistic, nostalgic reflection on our own lives that keeps us rooted in the past; it is that women's experience needs to be seen so that the world feels like a place where we belong and have always belonged, that the lives women have led and the lives they lead matter. Hence encouraging all women to draw upon their memories and use them to inspire creative work and fashion their own personal fable is also a feminist act because each endeavour by women adds to the diversity of representations of our experiences, mirroring women's lives in more detailed and accurate ways, and strengthening her symbolic world – saying how she sees the world and how she wants it to be.

On my wall at home is a painting of Irene's that I love, a white bull emerging out of dark blue background, giving it an otherworldly, mythical feel. The bulls are a familiar sight in the fields that surround Irene's house and regular subject matter for her paintings, but in the picture on my wall, the animal seems to take on another dimension, summoning up a world of centaurs, nymphs, gods and goddesses and so connecting it to the underbelly of ancient fables and myths that underpin the collective imagination. It's a reminder that our personal stories are always told against a backdrop of myths and stories that have helped us to make sense of the world and our experience in it as narrative – with a beginning, middle and end.

Hence the conversation with Irene and the work of Emma Talbot remind me that memories can be evoked through word, text or image and that attempting to confine them to one mode of representation would miss the richness and inspiration they can offer creative practice – and that the power of working with memory, through different media, is that it invites every artist/writer to recall things in their own way. Perhaps no single approach can do our memories justice but telling the story of your creative journey based on your recollections is a valuable starting point, as my conversation with Irene suggests. In her work *The Age*, Emma Talbot has refashioned an out-of-date tale, so that it reflects her concerns for the environment and how we live, and creates a new myth for the modern age, a new symbolic, in the form of the wise elderly woman and her labours to address the problems of the world. Within the Artspace of Talbot's installation and Irene's conversation, they offer a message of hope and a call to arms, to live and create according to what matters to you.

Creative Task: Your Creative Journey

Choose a friend, agree on a time and supportive context to complete the task, perhaps go for a walk together, have a cuppa somewhere there are no distractions, silence your phones if you can. Foster a feeling of openness and trust. Take turns to tell the story of your creative life, focus on just on the facts but also explore the undercurrents to your creative life, the things that motivate you. Be truthful but safe. Talk about three major turning points you can identify in your journey so far that feel safe to share with one another. When it's your turn to listen, be interested in what your friend is saying, offer some reflection on how it resonates – or not – with your own experience. Celebrate how they are alike and how they are different.

Bibliography

Barker, P. (2019). *The silence of the girls*. Penguin Books Ltd. ISBN: 9780241983201.

Barker, P. (2022). *The women of troy*. Penguin Books Ltd. ISBN: 9780241988336.

Beaty, R. E., Kaufman, S. B., Mathias, B., Jung, R. E., Kenett, Y. N., Jauk, E., Neubauer, A. C., & Silvia, P. J. (2016). Personality and complex brain networks: The role of openness to experience. *Default Network Efficiency Human Brain Mapping, 37*, 773–779.

Jung, C. G. (2019). *Memories, dreams, reflections. An autobiography*. Jaffe, A. (Editor) William Collins, Harper Collins.

Marr, V., & Moriarty, J. (2021). Reclaiming Stories: Invoking the Goddess. *Gramarye Journal, 20*. https://www.sussexfolktalecentre.org/journal/

Miller, M. (2017). *The song of Achilles*. Bloomsbury.

Miller, M. (2019). *Circe*. Bloomsbury.

Phillips, A. (2012). *Missing out: In praise of the unlived life*. Penguin Books. ISBN 978-00141-03181-1

Plato (201c-212a). Symposium in Sesonske, A. (Ed.) (1965). *What is art? Aesthetic theory from Plato to Tolstoy*. Oxford University Press.

Sesonske, A. (1965). *What is art? Aesthetic theory from Plato to Tolstoy*. Oxford University Press.

Smith, L. & Fray-Smith, W. (2022) (ed) *The Age Emma Talbot The Age,* Whitechapel Art Gallery; Thames and Hudson, pp. 36–37.

Talbot, E., & Von Stauffenberg, B. (2022). In Smith, L., & Fray-Smith, W. (Eds.) *In conversation* (65–81), Whitechapel art gallery. Thames and Hudson.

5

CREATING SPACE, TIME AND MAGIC MOMENTS

A Conversation with Grizelda

Christina Reading

FIGURE 5.1 Self-portrait (2020). Grizelda. Cartoon.

Grizelda's art, cartooning, navigates the travails of the political scene both past and present to bring popular and obscure stories from this world to life for audiences in an accessible, witty and visual form that is funny, clever and nuanced (see Figure 5.1). Established for over 20 years and well regarded in

DOI: 10.4324/9781003286042-10

her field, Griz even won the coveted prize of Cartoonist of the Year in 2018, (of which she is especially proud because it is voted for by other cartoonists) and has consistently worked for a range of well-known political magazines and newspapers over the years. Her work has been regularly seen recently in *Private Eye* and *The Independent*, amongst others.

Grizelda is part of Studio 106, a group of artists' workspaces in Hove where I also work. Over the years, I have watched her steadfastly sit every day at the desk in her small office with headphones on, listening (I am guessing!) to current affairs or music, gathering the threads of current affairs and bizarre news stories that lead to her wonderfully funny jokes – jokes she seems to wield in order to gently prise people open to another point of view and encourage them to laugh at their entrenched views, behaviours, and opinions. And perhaps only a joke can do that. Go into enemy terrain, lob a grenade in broad daylight and allow it to explode, resounding with a shockwave of good-humoured laughter.

Grizelda's imaginary world is brought to life using only a small A4 hard-backed black sketch book and a pen. The pages are intensively worked, densely packed with her small pen drawings covering the entire page in an economical use of space. There is a beauty in these pages, each providing a

FIGURE 5.2 Grizelda sketch books (2020).

unique insight, not just the ideas that lead to the final jokes but to the ideas abandoned along the way, a reminder of the amount of work that goes into producing a Grizelda joke. At the artists' open studios, which are held once a year as part of the Brighton Festival, she generously displays these books alongside the actual cartoons in her small working space in the corner of the studio. They always draw a crowd (see Figure 5.2).

Chris: *What is your earliest memory of being creative?*
Grizelda: It wasn't really an earliest memory because I was at secondary school, but I remember when I discovered cartoons and the joy of drawing them. That, I suppose, would be the thing to talk about. I'd stolen an exercise book from the cupboard in the science lab and I started – I spilled some liquid on it, that was it, and my blue pen made the ink come out green, and for some reason that was why I started drawing these pictures.
Chris: *Had you drawn before that, as a child?*
Grizelda: No, not really – not properly that I remember, but I must have done, because all kids draw. My parents haven't kept any of my drawings, they have stuff from my siblings but maybe I didn't … I don't know. Anyway, that was the start, and every few months after that I had to nick another exercise book because I would fill them up with cartoons of my friends, teachers and had started doing little stories.
Chris: *Was your style the same as it is now – that tightly packed exercise book?*
Grizelda: Yes, I suppose it was a little bit like that because the cartoons were all really tiny, I find it hides the fact that you can't draw very well. I've still got them; I've still got all the books; there are about 20 of them I would say. That would be the first creative thing that I remember.
Chris: *How did you encourage your creativity or what/who inspired it?*
Grizelda: The art teacher encouraged me; she wanted me to do a little slide show, but that didn't come to anything. I had to draw quite big, and it all fell apart. I'd done a cartoon strip, a cartoon book, but it meant drawing the pictures quite big, so because I couldn't draw big, the project got abandoned, but she was encouraging. And I got into trouble for stealing the exercise books. I got caught. A teacher caught me doing a cartoon, it was in Spanish class and she sent me off to the Head of Year, but he was very sweet, he said: *You mustn't steal the exercise books from the cupboard in the science lab, but do carry on drawing these cartoons because they are wonderful,* which I thought was great.
Chris: *Where did the name Grizelda come from?*

Grizelda: I completely made it up around the time when I was nicking the exercise books from the science lab. I started doing a cartoon strip about a political leader. It was Margaret Thatcher, but I called her Grizelda Grizlingham and her political party was the Grizlifications. I didn't know anything – it was 1979, I was only a kid – so I changed her into a schoolgirl, into me, and completely altered the cartoon, so that's where the name came from. The name came from Margaret Thatcher (laughter) (see Figure 5.3).

Chris: *Do you ever use your personal name?*

Grizelda: I had a phone call from the GP surgery, and they called me by my proper name – it's Catherine.

Chris: *Did you remember drawing or reading as a child?*

Grizelda: It's just … I don't remember. I'm sure I did do lots of reading, drawing, I don't remember that either, but I do remember playing out in the streets. A lot. That is my overall overriding memory – playing with the kids in my street, cycling up and down, doing

FIGURE 5.3   Grizelda sketchbooks from when she was a young girl.

stunts. When I think of childhood, that's what I remember. I don't remember sitting down being studious or still in any way.

Chris: *What was the route through to art college from there?*

Grizelda: Art college didn't go very well. There's a theme here because I am not very good at Art. You had to apply for a foundation year in Bromley, where I lived; there wasn't just Art in general, it was divided up into Fine Art, Illustration, Fashion, Graphic Design, but of course by that stage all I had ever done was Art at school, so I picked Fine Art. Absolute disaster – disaster.

Chris: *Why was that, Griz?*

Grizelda: Because everything I did looked like a giant cartoon. I used to go to life drawing, and it looked like a giant cartoon, and I wasn't trying to make it look like a giant cartoon; I was trying to make it look like real life. It was quite rough; everyone took the piss out of everyone but in particular they took the piss out of my artwork.

Chris: *How did you get through that?*

Grizelda: Oh, I was discouraged, I gave up any form of Fine Art, I still did a little bit, but it was absolute rubbish, and I just couldn't take it seriously. We were told one day to find a tomato crate and bring it into the college the next day, so I did this and went to the green grocers and I got a tomato crate and took it into the college, and then we had this sculptor who was apparently quite successful and well known, and I can't remember his name, and he wanted us to make a sculpture out of it reflecting space and time, some kind of abstract idea and I thought: *What the feck am I doing?*

Chris: *It wasn't for you?*

Grizelda: No, it wasn't. That was after A Levels, I'd done Art, English and Drama. And again Art – I spent pretty much every spare second I had in the Art room trying to do Fine Art and I got a D because I was rubbish. I've still got pictures from that time; I'll send them to you. And you can judge for yourself.

I left Bromley Art college after a couple of terms and then I got a job in a pub because that was more fun and actually it was great, it was like a real working men's pub and I was a middle-class girl from Bromley, and it was absolutely fantastic. I used to do pictures of the customers, big colourful cartoony pictures. I've still got some of them as well. I really enjoyed that. I'd do a portrait of somebody, and it would just come out all cartoony and I'd colour it in. The people in the pub loved them; I used to give them the pictures. After that I avoided work for another three years by doing a degree in English and Drama at Hull.

Chris: *Did you continue with your drawings at Hull?*

Grizelda: What happened at Hull was that I realised I wasn't particularly interested in drama because a lot of it was just silly – you know when you are doing drama exercises? I thought, *This is just silly*, and I wasn't very good at acting or remembering my lines and I wasn't very interested in the history of drama, but English I liked because I liked reading books. So, I just went out and found whatever areas of university life needed cartoons: the university newspaper, the union, and any magazine going: I did cartoons for them. I used to do the posters for the plays with serious themes but chuck in some cartoons. I just looked for things that needed doing, all the union pamphlets and booklets, handbooks that they gave out. I infiltrated into the inner circle of the people who ran the union and offered my services for free. So, they were like: *"Yeh, oh illustrate the union handbook and lots of advertising and oh and the newspaper"* and it had a competition to have a cartoon strip, so everyone was allowed to send in cartoons. So, I thought fantastic, great, so I sent in a cartoon strip about some students and they had three cartoons and they could not decide which one to have so they decided to have a competition. So, I basically went around the whole of the drama department and asked all of them to vote for me, put notices up saying: *Please go along to the* Hull Fire *(newspaper office) offices and vote for my cartoon*, and they all happily obliged, and I won by a landslide. When one of the other cartoonists said: *But she cheated! She just got all her mates to vote for her.* They said it showed confidence, good sense and zeal and they could have done the same but didn't, so Grizelda wins. It was quite funny. But I've still got that page from when they had the three cartoon strips and the other two are so much better drawn. I wouldn't necessarily say they are funnier, but the actual artwork is way ahead of mine as well.

Chris: *Wit and tenacity won the day then?*

Grizelda: Yes. So basically, I spent three years doing lots of cartoons. I did work as well. I scraped through my course; I got a 2:2.

Chris: *So, do you have an inner critic and how do you work with/against that?*

Grizelda: The inner critic is silenced a lot more these days due to the sheer number of years I've been doing this and that I'm able to go, *Oh just shut up*. I think if you have made a living from something for a few decades you start to think, *I must be all right then because if I wasn't, I wouldn't make any money from it*. Some days the jokes don't flow as well as they do on other days. Some days you are all day long struggling to come up with some jokes and then, in the last ten minutes before you go off and cook dinner, you come up with half a dozen, so yes, I am quite good at silencing the inner critic. If it does arise and I find it's affecting my work, I just stop, down pens and go and do something else and think life's about so much more than making a living.

Chris: *When and where are you most creative? What are the tools, the people you need?*

Grizelda: When I get back from walking the dog in the morning until about 2 p.m. before my brain starts to go to mush. Normally this would be the time that I would have a swim or a second dog walk.

Chris: *And what does your creativity need to get to the point where you buzz with ideas? Is it reading books, is it seeing things or watching TV, doing lots of drawing?*

Grizelda: Well, I suppose I will have done quite a lot of reading from magazines, watching the news, current affairs programs, reading current affairs magazines, Twitter occasionally although that can be grim, and also just feeling awake and alert and exercised. I can't stress how important that bit is. Like perked up, like I've got my heart rate going, walked the dog fast down to the beach and back, and all ready and set to go.

Chris: *So, getting some exercise first really matters to you? Matters to getting your brain going.*

Grizelda: Yes, it does. Because then the second session, the afternoon session after I've had a nap maybe, and a swim or a dog walk, then I sit down again and have the second session, which again is exercise, heartbeat going, all of that.

Chris: *What motivates you?*

Grizelda: I find it very, very tedious the way that people fall into their camps on either side politically, it drives me mad, anything that happens is interpreted through the prism of one's political views, and I like to take the piss out of that on both sides.

The idea doesn't come fully formed, it's prised out of the doodles in my cartoon books – I am sort of drawing different scenarios and people saying different things to each other and from there they turn into – some of them turn into – jokes. It's quite a long process and involves quite a lot of thinking and lateral brain usage (see Figure 5.4).

Chris: *I've always been fascinated by your books and how you go from the mad political world in which we live and come up with these really funny things which hit the nail on the head and involve a lot of energy. It's interesting to think about how you get to that point.*

Grizelda: It's not a quick process, and it's interesting that you pick up that it involves a lot of energy because it does, mental energy. It's magic. [laughter]

"Well, you're the only one who
thinks we're a sexist organisation."

(a)   (b)

(c)

FIGURE 5.4   Grizelda cartoons (2020).

Chris: *Do you think about your audience?*
Grizelda: No, not really. Obviously the jokes are for current affairs maga-
              zines so I'm aware that the audience is somebody who knows
              about the news, so for example in some ways Covid-19 and the
              financial crash were a lot easier because everybody knew that
              news item, whereas sometimes it's some small political nuanced
              thing that's gone on in Westminster, and you really do need to be
              an avid *New Statesman* reader to understand what the joke is
              about.
Chris: *What does it feel like when it all comes together and works?*
Grizelda: Excellent, it feels excellent. You think, *Oh yes that's really funny,*
              I'll draw that up, that's really funny, that will sell. And honestly if
              one editor thinks: *That's not funny enough to be printed* I just
              I approach a different editor [laughter].
Chris: *What are the things that hinder or demotivate your creativity?*

Grizelda: I work Monday to Friday and wouldn't think, say on a Tuesday, *Oh I don't feel like doing this today*, it's not really an option. There will be deadlines, so I have to. If I don't meet deadlines, then I'll end up losing my cartoon slots and not getting any money and not being able to pay the mortgage or buy food. If I'm feeling ill, I would need to be really ill, not just a cold but properly ill. I've had flu and chest infections two or three times in the last 20 years, which have totally floored me, so yes, then I stop because there is absolutely no point trying to work through it because the jokes won't be funny. I have tried it and it's just a waste of time. It will take coronavirus to knock me out [laughter].

Chris: *Can you think of a specific time or event when you hit a wall?*

Grizelda: I did some work recently for a slightly politically dodgy maga- zine, a very Conservative magazine, small c and big C, but I just thought it's the cartoon, not the magazine I'm working for, so I did something that I could just about get away with within the context of that magazine and hoped they wouldn't notice. I wasn't quite fulfilling the brief.

Chris: *How do you get round/past/through?*

Grizelda: Fortunately, I've been in relatively good health so that hasn't been a problem but when my dad died, I just couldn't be funny and decided to take a couple of weeks off. After he died, I'd fantasise about becoming a car parts delivery person because I live oppo- site a garage and I could see them pulling up all day long in these vans delivering car parts and I thought: *I could do that.* I seriously did, I looked up applying for it online and then somebody told me: *"Obviously, you don't want to do that full time as a living, it's just that you are grieving and you are having problems working"* – so fortunately, at that point a really good juicy illustration job came in that took six weeks and it didn't involve thinking up jokes, it just involved doing these lovely pictures. So that got me through it.

Chris: *What's the best advice you have ever had?*

Grizelda: There a few quotes that I remember people saying. Cath Tate, who runs a card company I've worked for, said to me once that: *"You are only as funny as your last cartoon"*. She only mumbled it, she wasn't trying to be some kind of great philosopher, but for some reason that always stuck with me. And then another one was a friend of mine who was a writer, who has died now sadly, I remember her saying to me that you must not let a thinking day, or a creative day become a reading day. It's very easy to sit and read loads of newspaper articles or current affairs magazines and sit in front of your cartoon book thinking: *That's interesting,* whereas actually thinking up jokes in relation to what you have read is the hard bit. That was good advice to be given and was passed on just at the point when I'd given up my part-time job and gone full time as a cartoonist.

Chris: *I recognise what you say about the tendency to spend the day researching, being absorbed by what you are reading. It's other people's ideas that are out there and the work comes when you interpret all of that into paintings or cartoons.*

Grizelda: Yes, that's the difficult bit [laughter].

Chris: *And you have to have the self-confidence to do that, a strong sense of self, and what comes through from what you've said is that you have self-confidence and that's been there from an early age.*

Grizelda: I wouldn't describe it as self-confidence on its own. It's more an element of arrogance [laughter], especially when I was starting out. People left, right and centre including my own family were telling me my cartoons where rubbish, saying, *That's not funny, that's not very funny, a crap drawing*, constant knockbacks all the time, and rather than thinking, *Oh god*, I thought *bastards, what do you know? I'll prove you wrong, how dare you say that? This is brilliant, look at it, it's excellent!* [laughter]. And I'd look at the stuff years later and think, *My god that was awful*, and I just couldn't see it fortunately at the time [laughter]. But I could see that they did have a point with the paintings I did.

Chris: *What enabled you to make the transition to being a full-time cartoonist?*

Grizelda: Just more work coming in. I got a few other magazines and news-papers; I just didn't have time to go to work, so gave up the job. I forget what I was earning, but I was earning the same from cartoons as I was from my part-time job. It was a good move, a good decision. That was September 10, 2000. My friends all take the piss out of me because I remember dates.

There are more men than women in the profession, but there are lot of women doing it too; you just don't realise they are women because they haven't signed their name in an obviously female way, people would just assume they were male. I deliberately chose the name Grizelda because that is obviously a female name, and I still get letters and emails from people saying 'he' and I have to say my name is Grizelda, for God's sake. It's like I have called myself Kevin or something. Yes, there are a lot more even than ten years ago, and they are just doing all sorts of subjects. Go back to the 1980s and there were a lot of female cartoonists but mostly concentrating on feminist points of view and specifically female things, whereas now they are just doing cartoons across the board on all subjects, so yes, it's changing.

Chris: *What does your creativity need?*

Grizelda: I suppose feeling happy, not having any major worry, not being worried about anyone, or your health. If you are worried about that it would put the spanner in the works. So just not having any things that are difficult or unhappy and just feeling up and cheerful, everything's okay. Trying to focus on the bright side.

Chris: *What's next creatively, Griz?*

Grizelda: Not anything bigger because if I draw anything bigger it's a disaster. There are quite a few of these cartoon festivals that I get invited along to, they say: *Do you want to draw a giant cartoon in the town square?* and I'm like: *I can't draw bigger than 6 cm so it won't work.* And newspapers, it would be lovely to work for a newspaper again, but they did not pay very well several years ago, and they definitely won't pay well now. I did *The Independent* for a while and it's quite stressful; it's a lot of work. And I won't go rushing to find something; if it comes to me, I won't say no. I like weeklies, just doing what has been in the news that week. I'm quite happy doing that.

Chris: *If you look back at your career so far what's your proudest moment?*

Grizelda: It's more an accumulation of having worked for particular magazines for a long period of time; I feel proud of that. I've worked for some magazines for nearly three decades; that's really something to be proud of. I did win the Cartoonist of the Year in 2018, and I was incredibly pleased with that, and it was voted for by other cartoonists, so I was very proud. I wasn't so pleased I had to give the award back because apparently, they give it to the next person the next year. So, I had to give it back [laughter].

Postscript

As a result of talking to Grizelda I reach the conclusion that having a goal and intention and a framework within which to pursue our practice is probably more important to creativity than we think. I often hear people talking about creativity in terms of the fun they have had or the insights or the wild ideas, the new skills, and techniques they have tried as a way of committing to their creativity. But if we were to take a leaf out of Grizelda's book and set our goals and framework for our days, perhaps might we not make a bit more progress? I would like to suggest that our notion of creativity expands to include this intentional and practical framework that adds to our understanding of the imaginative and spontaneous aspects of our creative practice.

Right from the moment that Grizelda nicked that exercise book from the store cupboard of the science lab in her school it seems to me that she set her intention to become a cartoonist, and there is a clear sense from what she has said that her decision making throughout her life has demonstrated an unshakable and constant determination to become the cartoonist she is today and to bring her art to the world. She has always been a cartoonist. Along the way she has valiantly fought back against doubters and disparagers, including her taunting brothers with a bloody minded triumphal, *No, it's brilliant, Look what I've done*, a reminder that sometimes putting your hands over your ears and refusing to listen to the detractors is an incredibly good move. Instead, Grizelda turned to those that encouraged, that invited her in, gave her space whether that was the friendly art teacher or the pub in which she displayed her cartoon style portraits.

Grizelda freely admits that at the beginning her artwork wasn't always the most well drawn or crafted, like the cartoon she submitted for the university competition and won by rallying her friends to vote for her; it's just that she wanted it more and fearlessly deployed whatever arsenal was at her disposal to claim the victory, gleefully putting her flag in the terrain she had conquered. It's a reminder to all creatives that alongside the imaginative and spontaneous aspects of your creativity, having a clear goal or intention and committing to it in an unshakable fashion may be just as crucial to paving the way for becoming the kind of artist/creative that you want to be in the world.

CREATIVE CHANGE

A Response to Grizelda

Jess Moriarty

Reading Griz's interview, I am in awe of how grounded her sense of her creative self is, where it comes from, what has helped it and what it needs now. She is calm, insightful, and the responses are intuitive and unguarded; she has nothing to hide. What sticks is how playful – naughty almost – her process has been. Stealing books to develop her craft, the made-up name and how she adapted the monstrous Margaret Thatcher, which informed her own alter ego. It is this confident play and quietly assured sense of self that catches my magpie-eye. This is what I need, what I have been waiting for. Lately my creativity has dried up after a pretty relentless spate of deadlines for (edited) books, articles and chapters came to an end. Suddenly, with time and space to write, I had nothing. The (wanted) pressure of other people's expectations had created an almost Terminator-esque approach to writing in me, and meant that I had produced a lot – I am not one to delay or muck people around; I always complete in time, but this isn't without its issues. In other writing, I have detailed my refusal to take any time off work and problematised this. On one hand, this makes me a reliable colleague and collaborator, and on the other, I tend to self-flagellate with work, never quite switching off, and this can be detrimental to my well-being and how I value myself (Moriarty, 2017). Griz talks about hardly taking any time off because as a freelancer, an artist, she has to pay the bills, but she also notes that when you are ill or stuck, you have to rest, recuperate; otherwise nothing will come. I have the privilege of having a full-time job where my sick leave is paid and still I don't take it, even when my body is asking me to stop and recover. This has been an ongoing battle with my body – my body not doing what I want it to and me punishing it as a result – and that hits home too. How can I use my creativity to make better friends with my body, I wonder? I read the section where Griz says she

DOI: 10.4324/9781003286042-11

pondered becoming a car parts delivery person in the aftermath of her father's death, when her own creativity hit a wall, and I reflect that lately, teetering on burnout has made me wonder if I could move to Ireland, start an Airbnb and run writing workshops. It's a flight of fancy – not a real plan – an imagined escape I flirt with, try on for size and quickly dismiss. It would never fit my busy life in Brighton or suit my happy children. But this 'what if' satisfies when work is tough, fantasy and reimagining is nourishing. Griz also talks about her experience of patriarchy and people assuming that she is a man – even with the name Griz – and how frustrating this has been. Chris sets a challenge to readers at the end of the interview to stake our claim, put our flag down and mark our space, and I accept her challenge! To story myself and reimagine my lived experiences in order to value myself as a writer and evolve my relationship with my body. This is the intention that Chris has demanded I set – the rest of the chapter is where I see it through.

Creative Rewilding

In *Wilding* (2018), Isabella Tree acknowledges the detrimental effects of intense dairy farming on the Knepp Estate and critiques the pressure on farmers to over-produce so that the public can over-consume, and how this is killing our natural heritage and decimating wildlife therein. She describes the decline in turtledoves, once the sound of British summer and now facing possible extinction, the effect of World War II on our woodlands and lowlands, and the impact of this almost unimaginable loss on the ecosystem at Knepp, but more broadly on our planet. Tree provides an insight into her own part in this massacre of hedgerows and biodiversity, and how the dominant narratives of produce and grow at all costs blinded her and her husband to what was happening at Knepp and what was being lost, in some cases, forever. Despite toeing the line and doing what the government asked, the family farm lost money until the point where Tree and her husband, and the land at Knepp, were almost ruined. Tree describes what happened as a sort of sickness infecting the landscape and her conscience. Tree's beautiful, heartbreaking, hopeful book reminded me of Frank's guidance for people wounded in body and voice: "They need to become storytellers in order to recover that voice" (1997, p. xii). In the past, I have suggested that creativity and storytelling can help with the essential rewilding of academia, providing a potential antidote to neoliberalism and helping us to decolonise pedagogy and research (Moriarty, 2019) – supporting the people and communities who have been traditionally alienated from academia to feel not just a part of, but centred in pedagogy and research. For me, the process of rewilding involves nourishing and replenishing what is already there, using something known and established but reviving and recovering it. As I begin this chapter, I have been feeling tired, worn, decrepit because of the increasing pressures in my workload as an academic and also because I have started early menopause. Using my creativity to reimagine and revive my sense of self helps me to value what was already there and also, accept my changing body – to celebrate this new chapter.

Bodies

My body is in a liminal space (Rivera et al., 2018). It is once again known and also not known to me. In the past, when I was pregnant and also when I had cancer, I used my creativity – my writing – as a method of inquiry (Richardson & St Pierre, 2000) to come to know myself and my body and accept them (Reading & Moriarty, 2022; Moriarty, 2014) and reading Griz's work, I am reminded of how my creativity has supported change in the past and feel sure that I can trust it again now to help me accept – rather than deny – my changing body.

Menopause currently affects the lives of millions of women globally and will be an issue of increasing concern as the population ages over the next few decades. Menopause is a complex time in a woman's life, leading to both physical and emotional challenges (de Salis et al., 2018), yet its well-being implications remain poorly understood, and this leads to negative impacts on how people experience menopause. There is a limited understanding of lived experience and a lack of visible stories about menopause in literary texts and the arts (Dillaway & Wershler, 2021; Manguso, 2019; King, 2013). Consequently, menopause as a stage in the life course remains obscured, and this can be alienating to those experiencing its various stages – certainly it has been a problem for me. I started experiencing symptoms of peri-menopause when I was diagnosed with skin cancer aged 39. At the time, it didn't cross my mind that I could possibly be menopausal; I was too young! And I attributed the night sweats, intense anxiety, insomnia and bodily changes to the stress of having cancer. But when the hospital appointments stopped and I got the all clear, the symptoms persisted. My sex drive vanished, my talon-esque nails (which I loved) kept breaking, my hair was unruly and my body ached. I would look at the stairs in the morning and my body would balk, suddenly unsure if my ankles would manage them. I went to see my GP, who suggested I might have started early menopause as a result of the stress caused by cancer – thanks, cancer.

My family really didn't want to hear the M word in our house. They had struggled enough with the C word and now here we were again – mum's body doing what wasn't wanted or needed – acting in a way that took me away from the mum/wife/matriarch they wanted me to be. And to be honest, I didn't want to use the M word either. I was in my early 40s, my kids were just stretching their independence and whilst still needing me, there was more space and time for me suddenly, and I didn't want to fill it with questions about HRT and oestrogen gel. That was for old ladies! – women in flowery dresses and support stockings.

Why I had this image of the stereotypical granny, I didn't know as both of my inspiring and glorious grandmothers wouldn't have been caught dead with a Damart dress or girdle, and the older women I knew as friends and those who I worked with would have deservedly roared at me for daring to suggest such a thing. But this is the image it conjured, the story I had told myself. Perhaps this is because the only menopausal women I had seen on TV or at the cinema have been very old and depicted as past it, problematic, mad. Even the fabulous Grace and Frankie (2015–2022), played by the brilliant Jane Fonda and Lily Tomlinson, whilst wonderful, were undeniably old. The first person I thought of when trawling my memory for characters with menopause was the Evil Queen in *Snow White and the Seven Dwarfs* (1937), which is the first film I remember seeing. I was terrified of the beautiful Grimhilde – also with long shiny nails like mine pre-menopause – who was so consumed with staying young and fair that she was willing to kill to stave off ageing. I can remember crying so much in fright when she became the toothless, grey, stooped old witch, that I missed the ending when all is well because the hag dies and Snow White marries a complete stranger. Ironically, I have recently lost two teeth because of grinding them at night, my hair is greying and my bones have started to ache – I am my own empowered Evil Queen, mutating into the inevitable crone.

Of course, the Disney film doesn't mention menopause, but I was immediately struck by this representation of ageing and change when I tried to think of cultural representations. Fairy tales are an enduring narrative trope in our lives, but this is understandably problematic when women in particular are often maligned and reduced to negative stereotypes – the maid, the (absent or evil) mother, the crone (Bent & Gavin, 2012). Rewriting these stereotypes can offer us agency and control, resisting the patriarchal tropes that have been used to undermine and repress women. Our creativity can instead offer up opportunities to produce work in the spirit of social justice and spiritual freedom that offers a resistance to dominant oppressive structures (Acker et al., 1991). As Celia Hunt (1998) argues, by fictionalising autobiographical experiences, the writer is able to move beyond entrapment in a single image of herself and to expand the possibilities for self, and that by storying the self, women are able to express themselves in a way that gives them permission to be different – different to the women in the stories they have grown up with and different to the societal narratives that mean menopausal women are either invisible or negatively old. Reclaiming and adapting established narratives can help women to feel differently about reductive tropes and also about themselves, helping them to gain a more empowered sense of self, capable of disrupting dominant narratives.

And at the same time, emotionally expressive writing has been studied to investigate its beneficial impact on people's ability to deal with emotional and physical stress (Pennebaker and Beall, 1986; Riddle et al., 2016; Jones et al., 2016; Houston et al., 2011; Botfield et al., 2017), and there is a growing body of research that argues writing about emotional topics and life events can lead to significantly improved health outcomes, such as physical health and well-being (Baikie & Wilhelm, 2005). In this way, creative story-telling can help us make sense of the chaotic and confusing (Gilbert, 2002) and restore our sense of self and our well-being (Fancourt et al., 2020) as it did for Chris and me when we used our creativity to find a way out of the stasis that cancer put both our creative expressions into – Chris unable to paint and me unable to write – but walking, talking, writing, painting to create our last book (Reading & Moriarty, 2022) supported us through the liminal space we were in post-diagnosis and helped us to accept that we are women who have had cancer. Trusting my creativity to explore and understand my lived experiences with change was also evident when I was pregnant with my son Reilly and I wrote poetry to him whilst he was growing.

4 - Small Bang

It started
with tiny explosions
near the surface of my skin,
your Luke Skywalker to my Death Star.

In the mornings
I stroke and prod my new moon
not sure where you have folded yourself,
if you're playing Sleeping Lions.

You stretch
to your full length, a king-size Mars bar,
poke my sides, checking for a weak point,
a potential means of escape.

More and more
you make your statement with your hand or heel,
and I want to call back -
I'm here,
I'm here.

8 - Cement

I am blown glass
my sides smooth as a fishbowl.
You slip through me,

perfect grains of sand
sink into my lower reservoir.

Already I have begun
to miss your heels
against my right lung,
your fists drumming
on the exit.

I am stuck between
needing to feel the weight
of you in my arms and
wanting you to remain
sealed safe within
your vessel of sinew, water sack.

But time is running out,
you are almost done.

Nine

I am nine months and eighteen days pregnant.
I am so full the waters overflow the bed
and pour onto the hospital floor.
The surgeon tells us the baby isn't coming,
she will have to cut me up,
she'll keep the stitches small.

Paul asks for five minutes while he changes
into the blue scrubs he will later steal.
I'm two beats behind on an epidural
the nice man keeps topping up.
I ask him to turn off Duffy,
I can't give birth to Radio 2.

No pain as the knife goes in,
I don't wince or cry as she prises me open.
There's a tugging in my groin
and Paul mouths *I love you* again and again
and I try to make a joke but I'm interrupted;
a feral noise splits the air in two.

And then there is no 'me' or 'I' anymore.
You are just everything.
And this *we made it* feeling takes over
and all the love we have for you builds up,
exploding over the bed, out of the room,
way beyond the stars.

As the titles suggest, each month I would write him a poem to mark and accept my changing body and this new life becoming. Poems felt like the right response and manageable whilst I tried to complete my PhD, work full-time as a new lecturer and look after myself – they were short and I could complete them in a matter of hours, unlike a book which needs more space and time. But Lorde (1984) argues that in order for a person to be heard, recognised and valued academically, the person must rely on prose rather than poetry. And for this reason, I have chosen to explore this new relationship with my body using prose and a process of storying myself as a character from a fairy story. This way of working is inspired by stories found in *The Bloody Chamber* by Angela Carter (1979), which retells fairy tales from a feminist perspective and also by earlier work, where a friend and I wrote ourselves as middling witches doing the hard, unseen, undervalued work in a world where lofty wizards sat back and did little for far too many kudos and too much power (Moriarty & Marr, 2019). We found that this playful and imaginative approach helped strengthen our friendship – partners in our own challenge to the patriarchy – and this seems the right response to Griz's interview, where she championed playing, adopting alter egos and navigating sexism.

I did think of using the Evil Queen in Snow White, but instead, I was drawn to a less visible character – hidden away a bit like stories about lived experiences with menopause. I chose a character in Red Riding Hood, which is a tale that has had several iterations since the time of the original tale by Charles Perrault in 1697 to titillate the court at Versailles, meaning that the original meaning is all but lost: "We pass it down from one generation to the next, unaware of its history and its power" (Orenstein, 2002, p. 4). The many adaptations of Perrault's story (1697) offer cultural and historical insights each time a new version emerges, from the coy little girl in the Grimm's story (1812) to the sexually empowered Red in Angela Carter's *Bloody Chamber* (1979). The story of Red Riding Hood visiting her Granny in the woods, only to be stalled by a wolf with (nearly always) improper intentions has been understood as multi-layered text, often pointing at women's bodily experience of virginity, menstruation, sexual awakening, sexual maturity, birth, death (Orenstein, 2002). For this reason, the fairy tale seems like an appropriate vehicle to tell of my own bodily experience with menopause. As shifts in my body occurred, I thought of the wolf in Red Riding Hood who changes from sexual predator to Granny to mother (after eating Red and Grandmother, the wolf is sliced open by the huntsman and the two women fall out of him [Perrault, 1697]) and lamented my own 'change' from young woman to mother to – now – granny? 'Beast Feminism' has linked women and wolves, in *Women Who Run with Wolves*, Estes writes that:

> Wolves and women are relational by nature, inquiring, possessed of great endurance and strength. They are deeply intuitive, intensely concerned with their young, their mates, their pack. ... Yet both have been hounded, harassed and falsely imputed to be devouring and devious.
>
> *(1995, p. 4)*

The wolf would have perhaps been the ideal character to reimagine myself as – it is synonymous with hair (its pelt), sex and also for presenting as an older woman at the end of the story, and these are all relevant to my lived experience of perimenopause where my testosterone levels have been affected as a result of medication, leading to downy facial hair, a shift in sex drive and – at 44 – a sense that I was suddenly ageing before I was ready. Storying my own symptoms whilst simultaneously detailing my lived experience with academia can help to make menopause more visible. In this way I can offer an insight into how symptoms can make working life more challenging for women in menopause transition or post-menopause; and how, in turn, working life might also make menopause symptoms worse (Atkinson, et al., 2021).

Much has been written about the symbolism of the wolf (Orenstein, 2002), and instead, I wanted to story a less prolific character from the text. Not ready to be Granny, I turned instead to the mother, who is virtually invisible in nearly all iterations of the fairy tale, a plot device who instructs Red not to veer from the path that will keep her safe. When Red fails to heed her mother, she is put in mortal danger, and so the message is clear: young women must do as we are told if we want a happy ever after; we must obey. In an article for the *Journal of Autoethnography*, reporting on a community project concerned with the increase in gender-based violence during lockdown, I detailed my own experiences of learning to please and obey (Parks & Moriarty, 2022) and the reasons why I don't want this to be the path my own daughter follows. So, in my reworking of this opaque character, her daughter instead tells her what to do and the mother is unsure of her own path and what direction to take as she struggles with menopause and patriarchy in HE. Orenstein has detailed how the wolf, Granny and Little Red are in fact "multiple identities in the same body" (2022, p. 241), and that is perhaps how we all experience our lives? For me, mother, academic, wife, daughter, writer all take up necessary space in the text I present below. By reinventing myself as a character, I am reminded of how we are all evolving and changing and that these processes are important, transformative. In this way, developing my story of the mother has helped me come to know and accept my body, and start to imagine that this might be okay. Change is inevitable – it can be hard and tricky to navigate, but our creativity can help us to go eyeball to eyeball with changes in our body, accept them and value the people we are when change occurs.

Jess's Red: The Mother

Once upon a time it was Monday. Again. The mother always woke up before her family and set to work making coffee, loading sandwiches into school bags and answering emails from the night before – messages sent in the witching hours when she slept and dreamt of work and what to do when she woke. Now in her 40s, the mother had become an early riser, content to busy around the house and make things nice for those who slumbered in her home and also in her working life so that when they woke, the world was a little easier because of her. She had learnt how to please people when she was just a little girl and knew that people liked to be pleased and so that's just what she did.

In the bathroom mirror, she saw a woman she sort of knew but who was also unfamiliar; she watched curiously as this strange person wiped oestrogen gel into her thighs and peered at hairs and lines that she swore she hadn't seen before.

Mother what big legs you have!
        All the better to go for long walks and raise that heartrate!
Mother what grey, wild roots you have!
        All the better to protect the environment with no nasty dyes
        and sprays!
Mother what downy cheeks you have!
        All the better to keep that chinny chin chin warm!
Mother what deep wrinkles you have!
        All the better to show the world what a happy life you have
        lived!"

"Mum? Are you all right?" The mother's daughter had awakened and was edging into the bathroom.

"And you missed one." the beautiful young woman said, nodding at a sprouting white hair. "I'll need picking up today, don't forget?"

"From Granny's?" the mother asked, "Oh at last, thank you, Scarlett!"

The daughter looked bemused, "God no! From football! We've got a cup match." She went to shut the bathroom door, "And don't you dare try and make me feel bad for not seeing her! Get my brother to visit!" but he had already left for school far, far away.

The mother smiled and rushed to get ready, putting on makeup and clothes she couldn't really afford so that she looked relevant but not desperate (she hoped). Her husband kissed her goodbye and asked what time dinner would be as he fled the house. He would return like clockwork on the count of 7 p.m., by which time the mother would have magically worked a full day, placated the children's woes and made the house spick and span with dinner on the table, all so he could enjoy his evening whilst she finished weaving spells on her laptop and hearing about his day. Sometimes it frustrated the mother that she was tasked with managing the domestic lives of all her family, providing emotional support and ensuring they presented as having a fairy-tale life on social media. She dreamed of telling them all to fuck off and letting the house go to rack and ruin … "Oh do behave," the mother's cat glared at her. "Who are you to moan about your life of plenty and privilege? You with your house by the sea and happy ever afters? Stop this nonsense and get on with it!" And she knew he was right, but this story and this life still seemed to not quite fit. Was it too big or too small? She dismissed these thoughts and watched as the cat settled down to lick its arse on her side of the bed; she gathered her papers and set off to work with a fixed smile on her face.

Conclusion – Happy Ever After?

The ending to my story – the ending so far; I still don't know how this one ends – resists traditional happy ever afters; instead, it is complex, and our hero is on a quest of self. Using my creativity in this way has helped me to feel more in control of my evolving story, my ageing body and enabled me to make visible my menopausal life in a way that satisfies – I make no claim that my lived experience is like anyone else's, in this story; it isn't even quite mine. Instead, it weaves the real and imaginary to create a text that seeks to make no 'truth' claims; rather, it holds up a warped mirror to what menopause can be like. The link between writing and well-being has been long established (Lepore & Smyth, 2002), and Hunt further argues that by fictionalising our own autobiography, the writer is able "to move beyond entrapment in a single image of herself and to expand the possibilities for self" (Hunt, 2000, p. 75). Inspired by Griz's creation of her moniker, I have given myself permission to story myself and use the process to understand and value my changing body – giving myself permission to be different, changed and seen. So perhaps the happy ending is apparent after all? But in my story, I think the crone might go on to prevail.

Creative Task

Re-story yourself as a character from a fairy story – you can use image or text to do this – try to consider the attributes of the original story that can help you to not just reimagine but also celebrate yourself in the retelling.

Bibliography

Acker, J., Barry, K., & Esseveld, J., (1991). Objectivity and truth: Problems in doing feminist research. In M. Fonow, & J. Cook (Eds.), *Beyond methodology: Feminist scholarship as lived research*. Indiana University Press.

Atkinson, C., Beck, V., Brewis, J., Davies, A., & Duberley, J. (2021). Menopause and the workplace: New directions in HRM research and HR practice. *Human Resource Management Journal, 31*(1), 49–64.

Baikie, K., & Wilhelm, K. (2005). Emotional and physical health benefits of expressive writing. *Advances in Psychiatric Treatment, 11*(5), 338–346.

Bent, J., & Gavin, H. (2012). The maids, mother and 'the other one' of the Discworld. In *Magic and the Supernatural* (pp. 65–71). Brill.

Botfield, J., Newman, C., Lennette, C. et al (2017). Using digital storytelling to promote the sexual health and wellbeing of migrant and refugee young people: A scoping review. *HE Journal, 77*(7), 735–748.

Carter, A. (1979). *The Bloody Chamber and other stories*. Vintage Routledge.

de Salis, I., Owen-Smith, A., Donovan, J., & Lawlor, D. (2018). Experiencing menopause in the UK: The interrelated narratives of normality, distress, and transformation. *Journal of Women & Aging, 30*(6), 520–540. DOI: 10.1080/08952841.2018.1396783

Dillaway, H., & Wershler, L. (2021). *Musings on perimenopause and menopause: Identity, experience, transition*. Demeter Press.

Disney, W. (1937). *Snow white and the seven dwarfs*. Walt Disney.

Estes, C. P. (1995). *Women who run with the wolves: Myths and stories of the wild woman archetype*. Ballantine Books.

Fancourt, D., Warran, K., & Aughterson, H. (2020). Evidence Summary: The Role of Arts in Improving Health and Wellbeing. *Report to the Department for Digital, Culture, Media & Sport*.

Frank, A. (1997). *The wounded storyteller*. University Chicago Press.

Gilbert, K. (2002). Taking a narrative approach to grief research: Finding meaning in stories. *Death Studies, 26*(3), 223–239. https://doi.org/10.1080/07481180211274

Grimm, J. L. C., & Grimm, W. C. (1812). *Kinder-und hausmärchen (Children's and Household Tales)*.

Houston, T., et al. (2011). Culturally appropriate storytelling to improve blood pressure: A randomized trial. *Annals of Internal Medicine, 154*(2), 77–84.

Hunt, C. (1998). *The self on the page: Theory and practice of creative writing in personal development*. Jessica Kingsley Publishers.

Hunt, C., (2000). *Therapeutic dimensions of autobiography in creative writing*. Jessica Kingsley Publishers.

Jones, C. et al. (2016). Feasibility and participant experiences of a written emotional disclosure intervention for parental caregivers of people with psychosis. *Stress Health, 32*(5), 485–493. DOI: 10.1002/smi.2644. Epub 2015 Jul 29. PMID: 26223511.

Kaufman, M., & Morris, H. J. (2015–2022). *Grace and Frankie*. NBC.

King, J. (2013). *Discourses of ageing in fiction and feminism: The invisible woman*. Palgrave Macmillan.

Lepore, S. J., & Smyth, J. M. (2002). *The writing cure: How expressive writing promotes health and emotional well-being*. American Psychological Association.

Lorde, A. (1984). *Sister outsider*. The Crossing Press.

Manguso, S. (2019). *Where are all the books about menopause?* The New Yorker.

Moriarty, J. (2014). *Analytical autoethnodrama: Autobiographed and researched experiences with academic writing.* (Bold Visions in Educational Research). Sense Publishers. https://www.sensepublishers.com/catalogs/bookseries/bold-visions-in-educational-research/analytical-autoethnodrama/

Moriarty, J. (2017). Soaring and tumbling: An autoethnography from higher education. In M. Hayler, & J. Moriarty (Eds.), *Self-narrative and pedagogy: Stories of experience within teaching and learning* (pp. 135–146). (Studies in Professional Life and Work). Sense. https://www.sensepublishers.com/catalogs/bookseries/studies-in-professional-life-and-work/self-narrative-and-pedagogy/

Moriarty, J. (Ed.). (2019). *Autoethnographies from the neoliberal academy: Rewilding, writing and resistance in higher education.* Routledge.

Moriarty, J., & Marr, V. (2019). Reclaiming the book of spells: Storying the self as a form of resistance. In Moriarty, J. (Ed.), *Autoethnographies from the neoliberal academy: Rewilding, writing and resistance in higher education* (pp. 87–103). Routledge.

Orenstein, C. (2002). *Little red riding hood uncloaked: Sex, morality, and the evolution of a fairy tale.* Basic Books.

Parks, M., & Moriarty, J., (2022). Storying autobiographical experiences with gender-based violence: A collaborative autoethnography. *Journal of Autoethnography, 3*(2), 129–143. https://doi.org/10.1525/joae.2022.3.2.129

Pennebaker, J., & Beall, S. (1986). Confronting a traumatic event: Toward an understanding of inhibition & disease. *Journal of Abnormal Psychology, 95,* 274–281.

Perrault, C. (1697). *Little red riding hood in Histoires ou Contes du temps passé.* Claude Barbin.

Reading, C., & Moriarty, J. (2022). *Walking for creative recovery: A handbook for creatives with insights and ideas for supporting your creative life.* Triarchy Press.

Richardson, L., & St Pierre, E. (2000). A method of inquiry. *Handbook of qualitative research* (pp. 923–948).

Riddle, J. P. et al. (2016). Does written emotional disclosure improve the psychological and physical health of caregivers? A systematic review and meta-analysis. *Behaviour Research and Therapy, 80,* 23–32. DOI: 10.1016/j.brat.2016.03.004. PMID: 27017529.

Rivera, M., Medellin-Paz, C., & Pedraza, P. (2018). A creative justice approach to learning. In J. Ayala, J. Cammarota, M. I. Berta-Avila, M. Rivera, L. F. Rodriguez, & M. E. Torre (Eds.), *PAR EntreMundos: A Pedagogy of the Americas.* Peter Lang.

Tree, I. (2018). *Wilding.* Picador.

6

CONNECTED CREATIVITY

A Conversation with Thomasina Gibson

Christina Reading

FIGURE 6.1   Thomasina Gibson. Copyright Phil Gibson.

DOI: 10.4324/9781003286042-12

I first encountered Thomasina one afternoon at the Women Over 50 Film Festival at the Lewes Depot cinema (WOFFF) 20–22 September 2019, an event designed to "celebrate older women in front and behind the camera" (WOFFF, 2019). A friend had encouraged me to come along to listen to women filmmakers talking about their work to round up the festival. Each woman was fascinating to listen to because of the stories they told about their experiences of making their way in the world of film and TV (and you can access these in the archive section of the WOFFF website. https://wofff.co.uk/, should you like to listen). But it was Thomasina's message on that day that as women we need to support and encourage each other in whatever way we can, that made a real impact on me for its generosity of spirit. When Jess and I decided to write this book, I immediately thought of her and I am very thankful that she agreed to talk to me about creative recovery.

> While I become me, I also remember you. This shall be a double gesture: you should be a bridge for me as I should be for you.
>
> *(Irigaray, 2000, p. 43)*

When I emailed her out of the blue to ask her to take part in this interview, she responded immediately with words of delighted interest that in turn boosted my own confidence and commitment to this project. Thomasina instinctively knows that even small gestures of support and what is offered (or withheld) in these moments can offer a boost for our creative projects, strengthening and reinforcing our individual and collective enterprises and creating a personal informal network across which knowledge and experiences are distributed. Indeed, Thomasina goes further, arguing in this interview that unless there are practical and legal reasons why we can't, that we have a 'duty and obligation' to share with other women as a way of saying thank you to those in our own histories who have shown us support and helped us forge our own paths (see Figure 6.2).

Based in Bristol, she is an experienced and much-admired filmmaker, producer and writer, and her office is the garden shed. At the time of writing, she was looking to secure distribution rights for her new family feature film, *We Can Be Heroes*, based on the funny and moving book by Catherine Bruton and starring Alison Steadman and Phil Davis. Thomasina describes this as a passion project which she "saw as a film from the first page". It is a story about how two young friends tried to catch a suicide bomber and prevent an honour killing and deals with the sensitive issue of racism in a serious yet witty and accessible way, encouraging us to look again at how we make judgements about other people. She has taken this film to the Edinburgh and Bath Film Festivals, where she deservedly received five-star reviews.

FIGURE 6.2   Shed (2020). Thomasina Gibson.

She is also currently producing a young adult TV series called *Toxic Treacle* and alongside her film and TV work, Thomasina has written (but not exclusively) for the *Daily Telegraph*, *Daily Mail*, *Sky Magazine* and *Film Review*.

Christina: *What is your earliest memory of being creative?*
Thomasina: Well, I've always been kind of creative. When I was very wee, like three or four years of age, I remember creating and doing lots of dances, and all kids do that. It doesn't matter, able-bodied kids, less able-bodied kids, they all dance and move. I remember my mum saying to somebody, *she's making up that routine*, and I would go over and over it joyously, until I knew it and then I would say to everybody, *right, right, have a little look at my dance*.

And then my first writing experience was when I was around nine years old, and I loved Gerry Anderson's (MBE 1929–2012 writer of hit TV series from 1960s: *Thunderbirds*, *Stingray*, *Captain Scarlet and the Mysterons*) and I remember I said to my teacher, *Miss McNiven I would like to meet Captain Scarlett*, and she said: *The only way you'll get to meet him is if you're a journalist, so write me an interview with Captain Scarlett.* And I did that. And years and years and years later I went to a fan convention, a sci-fi fan convention. Silvia Anderson was there with Frances Matthews, who was the voice of Captain Scarlett, and they had the actual Captain Scarlett puppet, so I got the opportunity to sit with Captain Scarlett on my lap – best thing ever. That's my first creative memory, my interview with Captain Scarlett.

Christina: *With dancing there is that sense of sequencing, and film has that element to it too doesn't it, that putting together that series of moves. Is that part of the way you work?*

Thomasina: Totally. When I read a book, I see it as a film, from the first page opening, all the way through that book. It doesn't matter whether it's a children's book or a heavy adult's book, it doesn't have to be fictional, it's the same if I am reading a factual article or journal, I see it in pictures, but I also automatically see how I would order the chapters.

Christina: *So it is a combination of a visual and sequencing mind which is very central to film. I did watch your trailer by the way. I got so excited; it is a great film.*

Thomasina: Thank you. Obviously, I am still very friendly with the author, Catherine Bruton, who wrote the book *We Can Be Heroes* (2011). (The main character is Ben, who lost his Dad in the 9/11 terrorist attack on the Twin Towers in America. It tells the tale about how he and his friends try to catch a suicide bomber and prevent an honour killing in a light-hearted way – encouraging readers to look at complex issues about how we see ourselves in a humorous way.) It was a passion project. I read the book. I saw it as a film, from the first page, so I wrote to her and told her that and she said, *Well, I'd love you to do it.* So, her lawyers gave me the rights to develop this film, and it has been a series of major challenges to get that film made, but I am really happy with it. We still haven't got it distributed. I am desperately trying to get the BBC or Sky to have it; they are asking for children's content but haven't picked it up yet.

But when I read the book and Catherine said, *Yes, I'd be delighted if you made a film*, I knew exactly who I wanted to act in it from the start. And I just wrote to them and said look, I've been in the media for years and years and years and never actually made my own independent film. I've sent you this book, please read it and please let me know if you'd like to be in it. Every single one of them got back and said, *Yep, absolutely.* Alison Steadman was on her way to South Africa for her holidays with her husband when she read it and then I got an email from her agency, *Alison says, absolutely she would love to be in your film and she would love you to use her name if you want in order to get some money,* and Phil Davis did the same thing, they all just said, *Yep, this is a great story, we'll do it.*

Christina: *There is a real sense that that was a step change in your ambition and a leap of faith to go knocking on those doors?*

Thomasina: Well, that kind of practical and creative thing together. I knew I wanted to create this book in a visual medium and having been involved in various roles from a chaperone to a director in various areas, I knew the steps that had to be taken to get it where it needed to be. So whilst I was really passionate and keeping that creative thing in mind, I also knew I had to get some names in there, use their names and their experience to get some money and use their experiences to get great performances as well. So, you have all these little strands that you know you have to knit together and then hope that it works.

Christina: *Yeah, so it is that sense of faith in your project as well.*

Thomasina: Totally, you have to believe in it, otherwise nobody else will.

Christina: *So, it feels like it's in a critical phase then, just waiting for that, for somebody to pick it up and run with it.*

Thomasina: It is, and you know we've had a couple of screenings. We had a screening at the British Film Industry for commissioners, and everybody came out saying wow, this is an amazing film, this is great. But nobody has picked it up, so we don't quite know whether talking about potential terrorists may be something people want to lay low about now. What we're trying to show is that we are okay in certain crises. I think we are a really together nation. You're always going to have pockets, sometimes larger pockets, of anti-anybody, but on the whole, I think we are really great, and I think this film shows it.

Christina: *Well, I really hope you get the distribution you deserve for that. What did you do when you were young to encourage your creativity and who inspired you? Who are the people who have been pivotal on your way through this course or inspiration?*

Thomasina: Thanks, yeah. When I was young, the people who were the most inspiring and encouraging were my schoolteachers; I had three fantastic schoolteachers, one in primary and two in secondary who encouraged every tiny spark. So I went through a phase when I was 11 to 13 which most young people do, of writing poetry. During a free period, one of my teachers asked what I was doing, and I said I was writing a poem and she asked if she could read it, which she did. Then she said to me when the class had finished, she said, *Why don't you just wait behind, I want to talk to you about your work*, and she set me little challenges every month. She said, *It's not like homework, you don't have to do it if you don't want to, but if during the month if a poem comes to you or even if ten come, one after the other, please can I read them, and would you mind if I commented on them?* And it was great, it gave me that confidence, some of them must have been dire, but she just encouraged me and the same thing happened later on in secondary. Where I come from in Scotland is not well known for its support for artistic endeavours, so the fact that I wanted to direct school plays and be involved in pulling them together was good. I love doing all the bits, I love getting the actors, I love getting the script, I love getting the artists, I love doing the admin, I love all of that, and I've been like that for years but one of my secondary school teachers absolutely encouraged that as well.

Christina: *What about your parents and your background? How do you think that has affected your creativity?*

Thomasina: My parents would let me do whatever; they were delighted. I was adopted and brought up by my grandparents because my mum was very ill when I was born and she wasn't able to look after me, but she didn't want me to go in a foster home or anything like that. The people I call mum and dad have passed away now and were actually my biological grandparents. They were fantastic, they were very much older, they loved it when I danced, they loved it when I wrote stuff. Whatever I wanted to do they would just encourage it. We came from quite a difficult area of Glasgow, the Gorbals, which a lot of people have heard of, and then I moved to Easterhouse when they knocked down the Gorbals so definitely not a wealthy (in terms of finance) upbringing, but my goodness the life experiences were super rich.

Christina: *Your grandparents sound like they were incredibly supportive of everything. I was going to ask you about your inner critic; we all have that inner critic. What has yours been like as you've gone through that journey and also where it is now, what does it look like, what does it feel like?*

Thomasina: I do have an extraordinarily strong inner critic, and I still suffer from imposter syndrome; you know when people say you know she's a TV producer or director I think, no. And when we have a Women in Film and TV get together or Pact (Producers Alliance of Cinema and Television) meeting, I'm sitting there thinking, *What on earth am I doing here?* I really am. So, in everything I do from a piece of writing to producing a film, I'm quite a harsh critic, because I know other people will be. But I'm not a destructive critic; I would think of being constructive. If I look at a scene in a film, for example, in *We Can Be Heroes*, it'll never be perfect. I can look at something and think, *That is good but it could be better here*, or I will think *It took me three weeks to try and set up, all the cars and the costumes for that scene; why did it take me three weeks, what could I have done to make that quicker and therefore save money to be able to be able to bring the production on?* So, I'm quite a harsh critic, and then I revise things so either I don't make the same mistake or improve the next time.

Christina: *So, it's based on experience then, especially around the practical aspects of the film. And the creative side, is that more of a gut feeling?*

Thomasina: Totally, absolutely everything I do is from the gut, and if it feels right then I'll do it and if it works, fantastic and if it doesn't, creatively I won't beat myself up because you know yourself as an artist, you'll start off to do a piece of work and then halfway through of two minutes into it something else will emerge. It doesn't mean that what you started and the idea that you had was wrong, it just means the muse has come in a different way.

Christina: *I kind of understand that because it's always a difficult balance when you set out with an intention to do something and you need to achieve it and stick to that goal, but then also your gut is taking your interest in another direction and that can be a difficult thing sometimes. I've actually learnt to park bits of interest for a few days sometimes so I can get the project I am currently working on finished.*

Thomasina: That's exactly it, I've trained myself. At the moment, I'm developing a TV series, but I'm also trying to sell *We Can Be Heroes*, so I have to be creative in the practical sense to get *We Can Be Heroes* sold, but my gut instinct and my desire to option another book to create that visual is there too. So, I've got two bits of my creativity working at the same time, and I have to think. *Right now I'm going to concentrate on* Toxic Treacle *(2012)* and not concentrate on *We Can Be Heroes* because then they get all jumbled up.

I am also writing a factual TV series now; it is about GPs and the NHS. It's a positive, uplifting, fly-on-the-wall type documentary with a bit of history of the NHS and also GPs in Bristol and Gloucester. So I'm doing quite a lot of research and then writing scenarios that we can film, so that's what my writing is at the moment. We have got a production partner and we have a distributer for tha,t but of course we can't do the filming at the moment because of Covid, but I am still writing for it.

Christina: *How important is your writing to you? Does it feed your creativity?*

Thomasina: Yes, it definitely does. And I just write things anyway I suppose, whether it's a short story or the other day I was writing – it was an absolutely beautiful day and I was in a new house so I'm discovering, just through the windows, new views and things like that so I just wrote a little descriptive vignette. I really, really miss writing and it goes hand in hand with film and TV because you need to be able to understand, you need to be able to feel what your writer is doing to make their vision work well. That comes from writing.

Christina: *So, in order to understand another writer, you need to keep writing yourself, is that what you're saying?*

Thomasina: Yeah, I think so.

Christina: *Ok, yeah, I totally get that, that really makes sense, thank you. When and where are you most creative and what kind of tools do you use? In a sense, you have partly answered that …*

Thomasina: Well, I have got a shed in the new house and in fact I was painting it yesterday. I had one in my old house too. I write best at night; at my other house, I'd have dinner and watch the telly, *Killing Eve* or *Line of Duty* or whatever, and then when everybody else was getting ready to go to bed, I'd toddle out to my shed. My husband had put heating in it, I had lighting, a desk and all my books and my laptop, Wi-Fi and everything. I particularly used to love it in the winter because if it snowed, I would be sitting in this really lovely warm place and foxes would come past and all sorts of things. So, between 10 p.m. at night and 2 a.m. in the morning I would say are my most productive times.

Christina: *Do you sleep at all?*

Thomasina: I do. If I am not writing I can't stay awake beyond 10 p.m., and as soon as I've finished writing I feel so relaxed, I float off, because quite often I'd be in my pyjamas anyway.

Christina: *I know what you mean about that time, because sometimes when you relax, ideas can come to you, so if you don't write them then they just keep you awake anyway, so you may as well write them down. Is there anything that stops you being creative? Is there something that demotivates you? What puts a cog in your wheels?*

Thomasina:	Stress. If there's a lot of stress going on in my life. I tend to be quite a relaxed person but I had a situation where my son (both my children are grown up) wasn't very well, my daughter was finishing her doctorate, we were moving house, Covid-19 hit and my husband wasn't very well and he was taken into hospital and with all those things together, I couldn't write a thing. I tried to sit down to write, to relax, just nothing.
Christina:	*How do you get back from that?*
Thomasina:	It just comes naturally. I know when I have completely destressed because then I'm champing at the bit to write something and that works. Another thing that puts a cog in the wheel is if I've been demotivated in the industry. So for instance, somebody asked me to write something for them and I was working away, doing all the research. And then out of the blue I got an email saying: *Oh no, there isn't a deadline, but you can carry on and we'll see* – well, what is the point? I really struggled.
Christina:	*It is very disregarding when people do that, isn't it, of your whole effort. And the way people explain that sometimes can have an effect as well. Have there been any times in your life when you've had big hurdles or knockbacks?*
Thomasina:	Well, the short answer to that is yes, there have been a number of times where there's been a massive knockback, and you do have to step back and look at that imposter syndrome. There was a situation with a TV series, a sci-fi TV series that we'd got the amber light for and as far as I was concerned, all systems go. There was a team of us writing together, and we were all having a great time, and then out of the blue we got this email saying this wasn't going to go any further because we have got too many things on our slate and you know if you carry on, we might not ever use it or show it so we're calling a halt. I usually write alone, but I loved this whole collaborative situation, and I really thrived under it, and it produced what I think is my best work ever. So then to just have somebody say, *Well there are five other ones that are better than yours so, we're just going to put yours at the side*, it was a serious, serious knockback. I spent ages thinking what could I have done to stop this, how could I have made this work, what is wrong with this that somebody else's is better? And you know there are fantastic writers and of course there are, I mean Russell T. Davies is one of the best writers in the world and, not putting myself down, but I would go with Russell's writing over mine for sure. So that the other side of it is you have to acknowledge there are greats and there are people who are going to be great coming up and you're

	somewhere in the middle hopefully. But it took me ages, nearly a year, to get my confidence back from that.
Christina:	*So, when you came back out of that process, did you feel bruised, were you careful with yourself?*
Thomasina:	Well, you do, you have to. I spend half my day saying: *Come on, you've had a knock and you are bruised*, and it does make you a little bit tentative, and you do just need to think about the things that you've done that have been successful and think about the things that you've done that haven't been successful and how you've come out of it. You need to be very gentle with yourself and look at all the successes you've had and even if it didn't work how you processed it and where you are now. That is a success, when you are not curled in a corner.
Christina:	*That is very encouraging. Do you have friends or colleagues or professional friends that you go to in those moments, and are there particular people you might rely on?*
Thomasina:	Definitely, a personal close, close, deep friend is Amanda Tapping from *Stargate SG1* and lots of other things. She's an amazing writer and director. Right from day one, very first episode of *Stargate*, she and I clicked, and we have stayed friends the whole time. When she comes to the UK she stays with me, when I go to Canada, I stay with her. I was there when her daughter was born and all that stuff. She gets all of it, she feels the same. If I feel really down, or equally if I'm really happy, I'll Facetime Amanda, even if it's 2 a.m. Canada time and she does the same thing, it'll be 3 a.m. and I'll get a Facetime and we can sit and we're very honest with each other and if I'm being an idiot she'll tell me, but super, super supportive of ideas as well, so if I've had a knock, I will go to her. If I am stuck for a bit of inspiration or if I'm just stuck, I'll contact her and just say, *What do you think?* And she'll say, *Well just take a step back and look at the end and see where you want to be with this piece of writing, see where you want it to finish if you can and then you can find the steps to get there*, so Amanda's great.
	And then I have got a super, super friend, Sue George. She's got nothing to do with the industry, but she just gets it and I can phone Sue, or before Covid-19 we would get together. Also, Dawn McCarthy Simpson is from PACT and is an astounding woman. What she's done for the film and TV industry, she constantly beavers away, super supportive of women, super supportive of people whether they have never done anything before or whether they just want to get in there. She's great at helping with finance and if there's a situation where I'm trying to get

something on screen or trying to get somewhere, you drop an email or a text to Dawn, and even though she is/was flying all over looking after British creative industries in literally every corner of the world, she'll always text back saying, *Right, it's going to take me 24 hours to get back to you* or *I've got 20 minutes now, do you want to phone?* She can do all that, and as well as that she does all this charity stuff, all these walks, all these climbs. She's got a daughter who is a train driver so when she goes down to London from Yorkshire her daughter is driving the train, which I love.

Christina: *There is a book in that surely!*

Thomasina: There must be, because quite often when the train driver says: *This is the train to London*, Dawn can sit and say – "That's my daughter!"

Christina: *What I've picked up from you was your generosity for sharing your support for other women, and it seems as if you've been inspired by other women and are passing it on a bit?*

Thomasina: We have to. I was inspired by my teachers right from when I was wee. I am duty bound to give it back out. What is the point in holding on to it? Share, if there's legal obligations where you can't share, don't, but in every other way, share. My friend Amanda Tapping in Canada, she supports a clothes agency for women in the industry who were either going to business meetings or were going to award ceremonies or something. You know as well as I do, when you're a writer you've got no money, but if you've got to go to a big meeting where your next job depends on it, you want to look smart and you want to look like you belong in that industry, so she and many of her friends in the industry, all different shapes and sizes, support this venture so you could take that business suit out and feel ready to face the world.

Christina: *All of that is very encouraging. What is the best advice you've ever had?*

Thomasina: The best advice is to persevere but learn when you're flogging a dead horse, and do it regardless. Give it as many goes as you possibly can, but if a whole bunch of people are all telling you the same thing, that doesn't mean give it up, but take it holistically. Think about how much stress it's putting on you, think about what else in your life you're not doing because you're pushing, pushing, pushing for something you think might be fantastic in the end. So, persevere, do not give up but learn to recognise when it's not going to work.

Christina: *And have you had a moment like that? Have you had times like that?*

Thomasina: Yes, I have. I was asked to write a book a few years ago for Titan publishing, who've been great with me over the years, and I thought it would be dead easy to write because you'd just go to everybody and you'd write what they say and that's that. But this one had quite a lot of complicated science in it as well, and I thought, it's just not working. I just carried on and carried on and they kept extending my deadline, and they would have carried on doing it, but in the end, I thought you're getting nowhere with this and the stuff that you have written is boring, it's really boring, so why on earth would you inflict this on somebody. And I just said, *Look guys, I am truly, truly sorry; I'm not going to go any further with this*, and they were really understanding and great and they let me write something else after. But I just pushed it too far, I had an idea, I thought it would be great, and they would have let me run with it, and then I just thought, *No it isn't you, it's not right*, they would have read it and asked for their money back.

Christina: *What do you need to be creative? What makes you comfortable? What state of mind or situation do you need to be in?*

Thomasina: Well ideas, as you'll know from your own writing, come out the blue anywhere but I need a spark, a spark of passion somewhere, whether it's a great view from a train or it's reading a book that sets an idea off that's different or there's a character in a book that's really, really interesting. So, I need a spark and things just blossom from there. I also need a quiet space. Now J K Rowling said she used to go to a coffeeshop when she was writing Harry Potter books; I could never do that. I have to be in a quiet creative space. Other than the odd gin and tonic, writing is the only thing that happens in that shed. That's all that happens in it, even if I'm not writing, I just sit. This new shed I've got actually looks down a little tiny lane, and that's great because every now and again a car goes past or a cat will go past, so it's just a quiet space and quite often, when I'm just sitting something will burble up.

Also, I do Tai Chi, because then you've got that lovely gentle movement, and my Tai Chi teacher says before you go for a walk, and this was long before mindfulness was famous, she would say do a mindful walk. Clear your mind before you start walking and then notice whatever comes to you, if an idea comes to you, an idea for writing, write it, and if an idea comes for a painting, do that, and if you think of a fantastic recipe or you think of a song do that, just absorb all of that chi and then let it back out in your creativity.

Christina: *So, it is important to you, Tai Chi and being fed. I did not want to dwell on it too much, but it's such a big event, but I'm just wondering how Covid-19 is affecting you and your work?*

Thomasina: So, on a very positive note, lockdown has been great for us, because we moved house and haven't been able to do anything else except stay in the house and go in the garden. So a garden is emerging from this building site, and otherwise it would have been three or four years for a garden to emerge, and we are blessed that we can go out in the fresh air whatever the weather, we can step outside the door. From a writing point of view, it has been great because the rooms are full of boxes and nothing else, I can come in, sit, and just write for the hell of it. So the pandemic personally hasn't been a hardship, but workwise it has because the TV series I was about to shoot, no idea when that will happen now, or if it will happen, because there are so many things planned about the NHS and people's experiences during the pandemic, I doubt very much that the production company and the broadcaster will run with it.

As a freelancer, again I'm very lucky, I've never really been out of work since I was 14 and worked in a bakery so financially, whilst I'm not a wealthy woman I'm not starving, but one of my team, my cameraman, he's amazing, his work died overnight, nothing coming in, no chance of anything coming in. So whether it's one single cameraman or a company, creativity will always rise though. People's creativity will still come through. Creativity will come out of this.

Christina: *I was thinking that, and I hear what you say about wanting to address what has happened during the pandemic, but I think people may want other things, so they might look at what you're doing.*

Thomasina: Absolutely! Have my film!

Christina: *So as to the future, what do you hope for? What do you think it will look like for you personally? What projects are you hoping for or more time for your creativity, your writing?*

Thomasina: I have been thinking about this over the past couple of days. I'm going to write my first independent script, because I tried to auction another book but somebody got there first. That's what happens, and again that was a massive knockback. I'd put a lot of work in, I'd got some potential cast members involved. One particular cast member, I'd seen her on TV and thought, *Oh yeah, she'd be great for this particular role*, so I wrote to her agent, arranged a meeting. When I was talking to her I thought, *Wow, your story is really interesting, you're so different from what people would expect*, so over the past few days, I've thought why don't I write a story or a script and present it to this woman and say, *Shall we make a film of it and see what happens?* I'm an absolute nervous wreck, I've never written a script. I've been in rooms where people are writing scripts, I've been in Canada with *Stargate* and *Smallville* and *Supernatural* and all that stuff; I've been in rooms with the writers and watched and listened to the process and seen that episode on screen. Anyhow, I've mentioned Russell T Davis before, we are acquaintances, I wouldn't say we're best friends or anything like that, he does answer my emails, we have the odd coffee, and he has given me some notes and things. I had an idea for a script before and I asked Russell to write it, and he said, *You'll be much better than me*, and I said, *Oh, come on* and he nagged me, *Have you written it yet, have you written in yet?* and *I said no I can't do it, I'm useless* and anyway I'm going to.

Christina: *Perhaps he will be your friendly critic.*
Thomasina: I hope so, I am going to send him a few pages and say, *What do you think, am I on the right course?*
Christina: *That sounds positive and a way forward and I enjoyed your shed! Thank you very much.*

Postscript

the other changes and I am also changed.

(Irigaray, 2000, p. 41)

I am struck by the extent to which Thomasina's creativity is partly the product of the conversations she has with others. These might be flickers of conversations she remembers from her childhood or more recent exchanges with friends and colleagues; all have played their part in shaping her creative journey. By cultivating these relationships with others, she has created a personal structure of support, a scaffold, a bridge into the world within which her creativity can flourish and be held when things go awry. The feminist theorist Rosi Braidotti (2002) argues that in order to account for "not just who we are but of who we want to become, we need to first draw a map, a living map" (p. 3) 'a cartography' describing the "social and symbolic locations we inhabit" and "the political and cultural forces" and power relations that govern our lives (Braidotti, 2002, p. 2).

Hence this cartography of our support networks matters, because it is a strategy that embraces women's personal experience and exemplifies what Braidotti describes as "sites and strategies of resistance" to existing power relations by circulating representations of experience between women and thereby strengthening the links between women individually and collectively (Braidotti, 2002, p. 2). New ways of working which stem from women's experience are reclaimed and developed. And so, what I would add is, as Thomasina has demonstrated, a strategy of using our personal networks of trusted friends and colleagues to support creative recovery. In our own work, Jess and I have certainly found that supporting each other through a combination of care and concern for our personal and professional lives has been essential to guide us through our own creative recoveries in the aftermath of cancer (Reading & Moriarty, 2019a). And this experience has prompted us to write about the process of supporting our own inner compass: an autoethnographic cartography through a shared process of writing, map making and walking (Reading & Moriarty, 2019b). And we would encourage the reader to reflect on and draw their own map and networks of giving and receiving support that they might access to aid their own creative recoveries.

As Griselda Pollock has argued in relation to making art, these conversations with our creative community enables us to "enlarge our capacity to feel with others and for ourselves" (Pollock, 2007, p. 176). So we need to support practices that nurture our capacity for reflection and change and follow Thomasina's example by finding ways to truly listen and support each other as women working within creative contexts.

Thomasina shows us that learning about ourselves and our creativity can be considered from two interconnected positions: the individual and the reciprocal, acknowledging that our learning does not take place in isolation but in collaboration with others. Drawing on these resources, our personal relationship with our creativity, our inner sense of ourselves as writers and makers and building bridges to others in our personal world, through mutual sharing of our creative journeys, is what will see us through setbacks, doubts and stumbling blocks, support creative recovery and make us better creators, stronger as people.

Bibliography

Braidotti, R. (2002). *Metamorphoses: Towards a materialist theory of becoming.* Blackwell Publishers.

Bruton, C. (2011). *We can be heroes.* Egmont. ISBN 140526524.

Irigaray, L. (2000). *To be two.* The Athlone Press.

Pollock, G. (2007). *Encounters in the virtual feminist museum.* Routledge.

Reading, C., & Moriarty, J. (2019a). Walking and mapping our creative recovery: an interdisciplinary method. In Moriarty, J. (Ed.), *Autoethnographies from the neoliberal academy, rewilding, writing and resistance in higher education.* Routledge.

Reading, C., & Moriarty, J. (2019b). Supporting our inner compass: An autoethnographic cartography. In Moriarty, J. (Ed.), *Autoethnographies from the neoliberal academy, rewilding, writing and resistance in higher education.* Routledge.

Women over Fifty Film Festival (WOFFF), (2019) https://wofff.co.uk/2019

SUPPORTING OUR CREATIVITY

A Response to Thomasina Gibson

Jess Moriarty

Thomasina starts her interview by sharing an anecdote about a teacher who inspired. Despite being an award winning and highly respected filmmaker/writer, she constantly praises and credits the people in her life who have supported, encouraged and pushed her creativity. This nod to her family, peers, friends and creative community is generous and evidence of Thomasina's human-centred approach to making – and to life. But this sense of a shared journey that they have all been on in no way undermines her individual success or triumph. If anything, the fact that she has the confidence to mention and thank her supporters and encouragers fuels my sense that she is loved, admired, championed, and as I read her interview, I find myself cheering for Thomasina and her future triumphs too. She talks about the people around her enabling her to navigate stuck places and knocks with her creativity, helping to remind her of all she has accomplished and how excellent her work is, and this is an important part of her strong self-belief, crucial as a creator in a competitive industry. This nourishes her along with the Tai Chi and occasional gin and it feels do-able, healthy. To maintain a creative community and use their advice, support and insights to feed our own sense of why our work matters is a mechanism that I can identify in my work with Chris. She is my critical friend – giving constructive comments on my work and drawing me out of work caves to engage with my creative practice; she is my inspiration – through our process of walking, talking, making and the chapters/articles/books we have made together but also because I see her put her own excellent art into the world in galleries and at events, and this makes me want to create work that connects with audiences and readers and say something about how I experience the personal, the political, the creative world, and she is my confidant and partner in crime – steering me when

DOI: 10.4324/9781003286042-13

I need it, giving advice, laughing at my jokes and reminding me that I am okay, doing my best, and that I am always more than enough.

The rest of this chapter is a transcripted (and edited) dialogue between Chris and me where we reflect on the book, our collaboration and what we know about our creativity now and where this might take us next.

Conversation

Chris: So, the first question that really arises is what have the conversations offered you and what reflections do you have on those that we've had so far?

Jess: I think for me, the creative conversations have been a really positive extension of the method that we'd already developed in *Walking for Creative Recovery* (2021), which was quite an intimate conversation between you and me that provided support when we wanted to reignite our creativity after it had wintered during and post-cancer. This book was meant to be a way of extending that method and conversation out to other people to find out about their experience of creativity, how they navigated any blocks and challenges, and to use their insights to reflect back on our own creativity, to see if we could understand creativity more broadly, but also our own creativity, slightly better or slightly differently. And essentially, it's just been really inspiring and enriching to hear about other people's take on creativity. I always think hearing about other people's creativity is inspiring – and I am very privileged as I get to hear about my students' creativity as part of my job – but hearing the women we spoke to talk about the things that they are passionate about, and the things that they worried about, and the things that they struggled with, and the strategies that they use to maintain and sustain their creative life, was genuinely inspiring, and there were some key themes that came out of it: about community and support, about dealing with inner critics and a lot about valuing their creativity because it has enabled them to live and sustain a creative life, even against the backdrop of cuts to arts funding. That ultimately it is possible, and more than that, that, it is important to live a creative life.

         How about you?

Chris: Well, for me the conversations made me appreciate the value of dialogue and the space that listening can give you to reflect on your own practice. It made me realise the divergences of practices and the idiosyncrasies of each individual's approach to their own creativity and how they've honed it for their own purposes, but also how they've made their creativity central to their life and have managed to organise their life around their need to be creative. For some people that has had economic consequences but it has also enriched their lives in other ways. So, there's no guarantee that putting your creativity at the centre of your life will bring you wealth, we knew that! – but it brings you something very valuable, which is a very secure sense of self and gives you a mechanism for an exploration of self.

What it did as well was that it moved our method on from being just one to one – you and me – to a more expansive process of reflection more on the nature of creativity and also the nature of other people's creative processes.

Jess: So, two things come out of what you've just said: the first is that focus on the other person and being attuned to what they're saying about their own creativity. And then also being invested in the new space that the listening opens up, where the conversation bounces back and opens up a space for reflection on our own creativity as well. And that is really distinct as we have found that space can enrich and enliven our research and our creativity, stimulating new ideas and work.

We also realised that for us and the people we spoke with, creativity isn't something that happens outside of our identity. Instead, it is often the lens by which we look at other things in our life: our domestic experience, our professional lives, our experiences with cancer, and so it's not like a hobby or something we merely like to do. It's something that is really important in terms of how we see ourselves and how we value ourselves. The importance of the dialogues is that they have given us or enhanced in us skills such as listening, acknowledging, challenging, supporting, and this can have mutual benefit for the people engaged in conversations around their creativity.

Chris: Yes, it can be a critical conversation but is it a safe conversation too?

Jess: I am not sure about safe because you never know what someone might reveal or bring to the conversation. All the people we spoke to gave us insights into very personal details about their lives, and this is important because, of course, you don't just want a cosy conversation, but you don't want it to harm anyone either.

Chris: Perhaps 'safe' is the wrong word. Rather the dialogues offer up a third space which is separate from the space of the two individuals. It becomes a merged space in which something new is created, and therefore the dialogue in itself is a creative act. The people talking let go of their individual positionality in the interviews, just enough, to create something together and in this way, the conversations extend out. And this will hopefully offer new connections and conversations too – that's what we wanted, wasn't it? For this book to be the start of a new – and tap into existing – creative community/ties?

So, what is your personal view of creativity now, Jess? And has it shifted because of the conversations?

Jess: I always had this idea that my great creative endeavour was going to be to write my book, you know, and instead I have come to value collaboration and not just looking inward but thinking about how my story connects with someone else. And that has been incredibly liberating and enlivening. It stops me from being narcissistic and instead, I find pleasure in creativity that is dialogic. And this fortifies me when dealing with my inner critic and enables me to think about how and why my writing can be driven by a social purpose and not just my own whims. I need the constructive feedback and challenge that working with others brings to get out of my head and think of my creativity in the world.

You know I have been motivated by the idea of being professor before I am 50 and seeing that as 'success'. I envisioned myself in an office with a big desk, writing great tomes, and actually I don't want that at all! I want to be in the world learning new things from new people via conversation and creative play. And that is a big shift for me. I don't care if I am professor or not because I want to do this work and I want to enjoy it. So, I have let go of individual success and moved into a more collective and connected space that feels right for me and my creativity. I see this as a feminist issue because it's letting go of success as dictated by a patriarchal hierarchy – synonymous with academia and the world I work in.

Chris: If you are letting go of this notion of climbing the proverbial ladder, with being professor at its pinnacle, then in fact in you're moving into this other third space which is a more collaborative, feminist space in my view. Shifting your energy to resist and challenge the patriarchy by doing something unexpected and going against their model of success. So that is positive and a form of activism.

Jess: I think so, but what about you?

Chris: I always feel like I flourish when working collaboratively. Whether it's in a conversation with you or with other artists, and I'm only interested in that. But of course, my own creativity is mainly focused on painting, which is a much more individual enterprise. I think one of the things that I've taken from this is to ensure that I am always painting what matters to me in that moment and currently I'm looking at paintings of my family and children and seeing that as being comforted, as a good place. But also, to see my painting as a dialogue between me and the painting, which I think I always have done, but this enables me to articulate my process as dialogic. I have also joined a few collaboratively based arts organisations, which have opened up new conversations with different people. So, I've been more outward looking. And that's a change.

Jess: Do you remember when we started the book and you were coming up with all of this Greek theory – Plato – and I was resistant to have creative definitions from men? But you said that we had to know the history of creativity and its misogynistic past in order to properly engage – converse? – with it.

Chris: Yes! Because our work is refashioning those early definitions – in the same way that people have gone back to Greek myths and restoried them – and we have played with them and value this as part of decolonising creativity. Which is complex because we are both white, heteronormative, middle-class women, and whilst we are aware of our privilege, we are also concerned with dismantling and expanding creativity to allow new ways of being in, and to push old ways of being out.

And I think it's worth just noting here the conversations we didn't have …

Jess: I think you are right. The book doesn't claim to have spoken to *all* creative people, and certainly we need to acknowledge that the book doesn't include enough stories from the global majority or LGBTQIA+ community or disabled people, and that is a failing we would want to rectify going forward. Whilst we didn't ask people about their colour or sexuality or if they had a disability before we met them, we could have consciously invited more people to talk to us who have been historically excluded in work on creativity. And that is something we have learned from here too. We need a much wider conversation that focuses on decolonising creativity, to find out what we don't know through our conversations and learn from experts.

Chris: That opens up a question around what we will do next and what steps will we take to remedy this?

Jess: So, we both write about our lived experiences and as part of that I think we need to problematise our privilege and open up spaces in our writing where we can learn from experts about other ways of being. The book has made me reflect on this and we would want any future work to be in the spirit of social justice and also a means to develop our practice as allyship to marginalised people and groups. By publishing/supporting/valuing work that encourages the decolonisation of creativity and learning from that work whilst being aware of the spaces that are not mine to take up. We need to make space for dialogues that can democratise creativity and we need to be sensitive and attuned to these conversations.

Chris: Can you say more? Be specific?

Jess: I think decolonising work can never stop. We will always need to learn from the experiences of other people and be open to new and other ways of being rather than problematising or demonising communities and individuals we know little about. I still need to learn more from members of the LGBTQIA+ community/ties, the global majority and to find out about disabled people's lives too. This will raise my awareness and enhance my understanding, and I believe creative conversations and creative work can offer this awareness. But for now, I need to listen and be quiet in order to learn.

Chris: I also want to learn more about the environment and how creativity can offer routes to change there too. How can we work ethically and raise awareness around the crisis we see playing out around the globe? Who are the artists placing the environment at the forefront of their work? I want my social purpose to be connected to how I leave this world and for my art to adopt a quiet activism. Who are the people and communities I can connect with and learn from to develop my practice in this way and promote change? And this will involve listening too and being motivated to act by what I hear.

I also want to make better environmental choices about the art materials I'm using, modes of travel I adopt and to reflect on specifically how my creativity is supporting the environment.

Jess: I always feel that my work is a kind of going against a Tory agenda and that we are both committed to being part of social change that is kind and inclusive. We want to evolve our creativity to be more socially active, so what will we do next do you think?

Chris: Our creativity often turns to something autobiographical – a personal concern or interest, but now we're starting to think about how it is in dialogue beyond the self.

Jess: I'm interested in the work storying lived experiences with menopause – the anxiety of having skin cancer meant that I started early menopause (aged 40), and so now I am applying for funding to do more work in that area, learning from the lived experiences of people who have experienced this stage of the life course including members of the global majority and LGBTQIA+ people in order to create a digital archive. So, for me, that is about taking a concern that I'm interested in, but also finding out what I don't know and learning from the expertise of other people and centreing that expertise as well. And I'm interested in what that new conversation might mean for my creativity and what I make.

Chris: Yeah. And maybe because I've had cancer for a second time, I look at the world and I want to do work about the environment. I have grandchildren now and I want to know what the world should look like or how it could look if we embrace change that can help the natural world. To create pictures perhaps of a world where we are kinder to the planet and each other. I have a lot of research and work to find a way into this concern, but I often work from a hunch about where my creativity should be and what it could be doing. So, it's about tapping into the conversations that can develop that hunch and fostering conversation with specific experts and places – be that Extinction Rebellion or Greta Thunberg!

Jess: I think we are both saying that our work will always draw on lived experiences – our own and the experiences we want to learn from – with a sort of utopian goal of contributing to a kinder, more holistic world?

Chris: Yes, our work is about humanity but as part of that, we need to be open to conversations about new technologies – artificial intelligence, for example – and to not be scared of innovations in science because it is creating change in how we live, how we communicate, and there are ethical implications that need navigating here. It is new territory I don't understand, and yet it is an essential part of our futures – how we communicate, how we create. This conversation is somehow inevitable. So, let's embrace it.

Jess: Perhaps that's at the heart of it? How creative conversations can support how we live well? How attentive listening and making can be part of that?

Chris: That's the conversation I now want to have.

Creative Task

Mezirow suggests that a deep process of critical reflection can lead to transformative learning (1990) and as you are nearing the end of the book, why not take time to reflect on the following:

1   Is developing your creativity to enhance your professional sense of self a reason for reading this book? If so, why and how would you imagine this taking shape?
2   Do you make time and space outside of your work and/or personal commitments to be creative?
3   What does your creative space and time currently look like?
4   What supports this process (time and space, mentor, deadlines, etc.)?
5   Where are the overlaps between your creativity and professional and/or personal life?
6   Where and when is the dedicated time and space for you and your creativity?
7   How can you value and enhance this space and time?

Read the reflection back and think about what you can take forward to support and evolve your creative life – professionally and/or personally.

Bibliography

Mezirow, J. (1990). How critical reflection triggers transformative learning. In J. Mezirow, et al. (Eds.), *Fostering critical reflection in adulthood* (pp. 1–20). Jossey Bass.

7

MAKING YOUR CREATIVE LIFE WORK AND MAKING WORK YOUR CREATIVE LIFE

A Conversation with Lisa Norman

Jess Moriarty

Lisa Norman is the founder and director of Lout Productions, which promotes music events all over Brighton, making new and established artists widely accessible and cementing Brighton's reputation as a cultural and good-time mecca. Lisa has played key roles in organising the legendary Brighton Pride and the innovative Wilderness Festival whilst also leading her team at Lout to produce The Great Escape Festival, now in its 17th year and growing in popularity, causing Steve Lamacq to call it: 'The Cannes of the music world'. The Great Escape is imaginative and inclusive and kick-starts summer in the city with a roar. Arranging highly acclaimed events and bringing music to the masses has enabled Lisa to make her creative passion her work – something many of us aspire to. What helps her achieve this and to such an incredibly high standard?

I wonder how Lisa has maintained a balance and what advice she has for people who want to make their creative life their work. At the time of the interview in 2019, Covid-19 had put paid to nearly all live music events, and one might have expected Lisa to be resting or despairing, but she was neither. Her energy and drive inspire, and Lisa has also managed to find the time to revive the local school's Parent-Teacher Association (PTA,) which is now run to the kind of level any CEO would be envious of.

Juggling the school-run and organising events that create lifelong memories for thousands is just a normal day, so does she still find time for creative space that nourishes and motivates her? And if so, how?

Lisa: I guess I've always been creative in lots of different ways, I suppose, and I still have a very kind of hands-on approach. I do like to make a little bit of mess and make things that aren't related to my career – like

DOI: 10.4324/9781003286042-14

making soap this weekend or you know, baking and probably always have done, I think. Right from being a child I suppose I was always wanting to be doing things, not entirely academic, more of a kind of maker-doer, make a bit of mess, try and experiment type of person.

Jess: *I think that part is really important. One of the things that I realised is that I don't always take enough risks, and I don't like to play and I don't do the things that might make me look vulnerable or stupid. What encouraged and inspired that kind of playfulness or willingness to experiment?*

Lisa: Definitely my mum. Definitely. Yeah, I would say it all comes from my mum, and all of my early memories are baking, making, sticking, gluing, you know, *Let's make these …* and it's funny because some people are not allowed and some parents are, you know when they're little, *Oh God, don't get the paints out because they'll make a mess*, whereas I'm like *Oh, it'll be all right, we'll just tidy up, we'll just do this*, and so yeah, so it's definitely come from my mum the creativity, and the freedom to just be allowed to do it as well and you know push it a little bit, I suppose.

Jess: *Was music part of that as well?*

Lisa: Music definitely came in my teens. I remember stealing my brother's cassettes and listening to them while I was in the bath. So, I think early creativity was more about making a mess and exploring stuff, and I think certainly from early teens, it became very much about music and you know discovering music and things that you could relate to, I guess, as a teen.

Jess: *With that making a mess thing, do you feel like that's something that you have been able to thread right the way through? With your kids, but also in your professional work, do you feel like you are willing to take risks?*

Lisa: I think it's my outlet actually. Because in my career, I bring other people in to do those bits that are much better at it than me, the creative and design aspects, so it's probably the opposite actually. The making and creating and doing is what I like to do when I'm not working. That's my outlet to get away from the spreadsheets and the meetings and the emails.

Jess: *What you do is so creative in terms of what it does for Brighton as a city, and for the people, that on one hand it's a very creative job, but on the other hand it must take focus and precision and huge organisation as well, so the mess and play and the risk kind of comes outside of that?*

Lisa: Yeah, and I think you have some days when you forget that it's a creative career because you're so immersed in it. I really like the summer, in summer we have all our planning and dreaming and what about this? and what about this? And it's a really nice time of year to be creative and feel creative. I love the debriefing and the planning stages because you have a lot of headspace to feel it, I suppose. Then once you get into proper event management, you're past that lovely, fluffy stage of dreaming – floating stages in the sea and all these wonderful possibilities and you're into the kind of grit.

I think it's probably only then when you get to the delivery that you go oh yeah, hold on, we've done this and you remember what you were planning and what you were designing and creating, but there is definitely a period where it doesn't feel like that [laughs].

Jess: *With that idea of dreaming, have you always felt like you've given yourself permission to dream or carved out space and time to have that kind of lucid thinking or dream space?*

Lisa: Yeah, I think I definitely need that in the calendar. For me, it's very much an annual thing. It peaks and troughs throughout the year as opposed to throughout the week, and I definitely need that time of just being able to think straight. Like I say, in the summer usually post–Great Escape, we'll have a bit of time off and that's really important. I've got a lot of colleagues that roll from one event to the next event to the next event to the next event and I don't think I could do that. I think I need to have that space to think and, you know, and start again really.

Jess: *Do you remember always being like that or is that something that you've adapted into your practice as you've got more experience?*

Lisa: I think it's something I've learnt to do. And I think certainly since having kids, you have to change the way you work and you realise you can't do everything all the time. Definitely before I had kids I would have just carried on and on and on and worked and worked and worked and worked, and I think now I really appreciate the downtime and I see the benefits of the downtime as well.

Jess: *Yeah, that really rings true with me as well. And the summer does seem to be that sort of magical time where everything kind of goes on hold for a bit too.*

Lisa: Yeah. Those six weeks are a blessing and a curse really, aren't they [laughs]?

Jess: *I don't think I did see them as a blessing when they were really small, but more and more now, I see it as a huge blessing and now I feel like I'm getting to the other side, and I'm starting to think they're not going to want this six weeks with me much longer you know – is this my last year, or maybe two more years – before they start going, "can you just drop me off somewhere?" or "can you give me some money?" so it sort of feels that summer is still a magical time if you like.*

Lisa: I love that period. It's a different pace of life, and I can fit my work into my working hours, which is always a luxury. I've definitely learnt to do that.

Jess: *Do you have an inner critic, and how do you work with or against that?*

Lisa: Ah, yeah, I definitely have those 'I can't do this' moments frequently, but I'm very positive generally and like to think I'm quite resilient. I always try to see the positives and keep strong and keep pushing on and sort of remembering the goal. I do have the odd wobble, but usually, interestingly, when I'm not really busy, like post-Christmas, I start to think, *Oh, I don't think I can do this anymore*, but when I'm really, really busy and find it hard again just juggling home life and work, you get that point where you just feel like you're doing everything badly [laughs]. And then I do have those days and just think, *I don't think I can, I don't think I can* – so I guess my doubts come more in my ability to juggle everything I've taken on, as opposed to my ability to be able to do my job I suppose. I have quite a strong belief that I'm on the right path and I know what I'm doing when it comes to my career, but there's definitely moments in life when I just think, *I'm not sure, I'm doing this right …*

Jess: *And that resilience, that kind of positive outlook, are they crucial features when leading a team with a difficult task? I mean, organising a city-wide festival in all those venues with all those people and all that health and safety, I suppose people are looking at you to say: we can do this! This is all going to be okay!*

Lisa: Yeah, I think so. Everyone has different styles and different ways of working, but for me it's very much at the forefront of what I do and how I lead a team and how I believe we can achieve something is just to have that positivity. Remembering your values and remembering that we can do this. I work with a fantastic team that come onboard year after year, so we know each other very well, and everyone has their wobbles at different times, but it's really important to pick other people up and re-focus them.

Jess: *There are two things I wanted to come back to – when you said about how actually it's that quiet time when your inner critic is louder, I feel like that too – when I have time and space that's when I start thinking, I can't do this, I've got too much on, how am I going to get through – when you're busy, you don't have time to listen to the voice telling you that you can't do it and stuff?*

Lisa: Yeah. I think you suppress it and you push it away. You hide it somewhere; you pop it back in its box [laughs]. I've done The Great Escape for 15 years, and I've promoted shows for 25 years, but I was offered two very different roles in the last year – both of which I thought, *I can't do that, I can't do it* – and the two different people that were offering me roles you know were saying, *We'd love you to come and do this, we think you're the best person to do this*, and I was just saying to my husband, *I can't, I don't think I can do this*, and I felt like a fraud. I felt like people thought I was really good at something, but actually I'm not. It's just a bluff [laughs]. It's amazing how your mind can –and both of those contracts I've taken them on and I've done an okay job – say, *I can't do that* [laughs].

Jess: After I had Arla [my daughter], I was thinking about going back to work, and I was just thinking, *this is ridiculous*, why am I doing this? I'm never going to be able to do this, and then I felt guilty because I was spending my maternity leave worrying about going back to work.
The other thing I wanted to talk about – you said about how you thought one of the most important things was that ability to pick people up when they hit walls. I think that's really crucial in somebody leading a team, but do you find it sometimes means that because you're giving time to other people, you don't give it to yourself?

Lisa: I think I'm always guilty of not giving myself enough time. I think I put myself at the bottom of the pile quite often and I think: *I've got to do this for the kids, I've got to do this for home, I've got to do this for them, I've got to …* and to be honest, I think I probably always will. I volunteer in my downtime – I do things for school, I do things for the football club, I feel like I always have to give something, and I get a lot of satisfaction from that, but I think the downside is that you do put yourself you know at the bottom sometimes. I am definitely guilty of that.

Jess: Yeah, and it's not a small volunteer thing, is it? You are leading huge projects in the school as well, so I mean it's full-time job in itself, isn't it?

Lisa: I see things and I just think, *Oh I could do that*, or *I could help with that*. I've done the same now with the football club, and I see little gaps and I just think, hold on a minute, *I could do your Twitter, I could do that better than you're doing it, you need my help!* and I sort of muscle my way into these things that I just probably shouldn't [laughs]. I can't help myself.

Jess: They're never going to let you leave the PTA. That is for sure! When you have those moments of doubt, do you have people that you can go to, or do you have strategies for those moments?

Lisa: I have a couple of really good people around me. My husband's one, and I've also got a very good friend and colleague that I work with a lot on events, and she's an amazing mentor. She probably wouldn't call herself that, but she's just incredible and she's my go-to. She runs a huge company and works on huge events, bigger than the events I work on, and some of the same events as well. But professionally, she's my go-to when I have those self-doubts and I don't want them out too far and wide because otherwise other people will start going, *Oh yeah, you're right* [laughs]. So, I think you have to keep them very close to the heart and at home I have proper wobbles where I'll just be like: *I can't do this anymore,* and then that's passed. Then professionally, I have one colleague in particular, where I can pick up the phone and she will literally just knock me back into shape and send me back out there to do it. And she's always right. And you know, I do the same for her. We have these calls, we text each other saying, *Do you need one of those chats?* And it's really critical to set you back on the right track.

I think it's grown organically through friendship, through working together and mutual respect for each other.

Jess: *That's a really interesting way to use a mentor. When and where are you most creative? Do you have a room of your own, or a space of your own …?*

Lisa: I'll show you. [shows office] This is my little office, but actually it's got a Play Station and a sofa over there. So, it's supposed to be my lovely little office and it usually is during the day until my son gets home and then it becomes, you know, gaming den. I split my time between an office in town and working from home. I think it's really important to have some sort of nook to work, whether it's the kitchen table or somewhere that you're comfortable working.

Jess: *Is a change of landscape important to you as well? In terms of having professional ordered meetings, being present for people and then having some wild space if you like?*

Lisa: Yeah, definitely, I think it's a really big part of me really. When you run your own business, your work never stops, there's always an email, there's always somebody that needs something, there's always a plan to be written, so it's really important, that escapism or holidays. And I don't mean two weeks in the Caribbean, I mean just one night that's not here, maybe camping or a change of scenery, being away from home, whether it's just for a day, a weekend or a few days, just to – not switch off completely – but just to change the thought processes, I guess.

Jess: *Is lockdown a time you think you're going to remember as when you had to bounce back creatively?*

Lisa: I think this is probably on a par with having kids, as you mentioned, in a very strange way it's not like having kids! But I really felt I was winning for the first time ever probably, I'd taken on a new contract, I was managing to get all my work done. I'd sorted my schedule, my workdays, my office days, my London days, there was food in the fridge, the kids were fine. I think I felt I was winning before all of this kicked off, and obviously it does knock you for six, because you're not quite sure where you're going again. I do struggle a bit whenever I take any time off, I struggle if I come back after Christmas, but certainly from having kids. I only took a couple of weeks maternity leave from both kids because I run my own business and it doesn't stop. But in some ways, I think that's a benefit because then it's harder to get going again. So, this feels a little bit like that quiet time. You've got to scoop yourself back up again and remember what you were doing and have the enthusiasm to do it as well because sometimes it's hard to get yourself going again mentally; sometimes you just don't want to bother.

Jess: *What are the things you draw on to get that enthusiasm back? Is it that you know you have a team relying on you or have you got strategies that help you galvanise yourself in those times?*

Lisa: I was on a phone call, literally just before I came on here, with somebody talking about a new project and a new idea. As soon as I reconnect with the people I work with, you very quickly fall back into that place and remember your place again, but it's quite easy to go off in your own little bubble and struggle to come back again.

Jess: *How do you juggle so many projects, not just your professional work, but the other things you've said are side-lines, but I sort of see as a full-time job? How do you do all that and cope with the pressure to be productive that there is at the moment, say whether that's baking with your kids or painting with your kids or doing yoga or whatever as well? Do you think you can navigate that quite successfully or does it sometimes feel overwhelming?*

Lisa: I mean, I thrive on being busy. I do my best work and my best parenting and my best everything when I'm busy because if I'm busy, I'm more organised. I'm quite good at scheduling my time and kind of saying, *Right, I'm going to get this done*; I'm a big fan of lists, I'm a big fan of Trello, of organising, I prefer to be busy. If I have nothing apart from one job, I probably won't do it, if I have ten jobs on, I will probably do nine of them.

Jess: *And are there any other things, apart from staying busy, that hinder or motivate your creativity?*

Lisa: Getting out in the fresh air definitely motivates. Stepping away from the treacle I'm usually wading through helps, walking, gardening definitely gives me that strength, I guess. You know yesterday I had to go out in the rain and weed the front garden just to get away from everybody and pretend I was really enjoying it. But I just stood out there and I had a cup of coffee and half an hour was all I needed. Half an hour away from everybody just to be able to come back in and carry on, and I think it's really important to have that break and that space in the fresh air as well – whatever the weather – we took the kids out in the rain for an hour and a half yesterday just because we had to, they don't thank me for it.

Jess: *They will do one day, that's what I keep telling mine*: one day you're going to thank me for this!

Lisa: Yeah, they do by the end, they love it, but the moaning for 20 minutes: *Oh, it's raining, do we have to go through that field again?*

Jess: *You talked about having a mentor, what's the best advice you've ever been given?*

Lisa: Probably, the best advice from a working perspective, was years and years ago, I think it was in year two of the Great Escape. I manage a very big team onsite at the Great Escape, about 180 people and about 300 volunteers, pretty bonkers, and I remember the fire alarms were going off in Horatio's Bar on the end of the pier. One of these situations that always crops up, and I had to run down there, physically run down there and deal with it. It was all fine, there was no fire, it was the smoke machine, blah, blah, blah, and I ran down there, and I remember my old line manager at the time, one of the directors, took me to one side and bought me a coffee. He could see that I was, you know, literally firefighting, and he said to me, *The secret of your success will be in your delegation* – and it's always stuck with me, because I'm very much, probably the same as a lot of people, I like to do everything, do it my way. I like to think I can do everything in the entire world and it's really hard to let go, to trust other people to do things you think you could probably do better in half the time. Learning to delegate is a really tricky thing, but I do think it's worth the time and effort you put into it because it's very easy to go, *Oh give it here, I'll do it*, because you can see it's quite difficult or you can see people making mistakes or not doing something the way you want it done. But I think that once you learn to pass things over and trust people to do things the way you'd like it done, with their own stamp on it, I think that's how you grow really and that's a really important little piece of advice that I would pass on to anybody. I used to be at death's door before we'd go into an event, just from being up all night, then up at 5 a.m. I couldn't sleep, I'd be working, finishing spreadsheets off, really, really stressed, and now as we approach the event, my husband goes, *There's something really weird, like, what's wrong with you?* Now, I wrap up my work at a sensible time, I can sleep at night, I'm not stressed, and he's just like, *Something has really changed*, and I do think that's what it is. It gives you that calmness and that clarity, you can think straight, everyone is doing the things they should be doing and you can rise above it all and look at the bigger picture, deal with the things that are really important as opposed to getting yourself immersed in all the detail. So, I think that's the single most important thing I've been told in terms of my career.

Jess: *I think that's a really good one. My thing is starting things. So, I'll say to someone: You start it, and then if they don't start it, I'll just start it. But I should just leave it alone.*

Lisa: I've got my own one, my own motto that I've devised, and I tell people all the time, it's just that the world doesn't end if you take a day off. Years ago, I was dreadful, I was an absolute workaholic. I guess probably from what you see of me doing 50,000 things, I still am, but I'm a real stickler for work-life balance now, and I've got other mum friends who are really busy working in events going, *How do you do it*, and you know what, take a day off, literally the world does not end. Go on that holiday or do whatever, because your work is still going to be there, nothing is going to change, and I think it's a really difficult one that you have to learn for yourself, but once you do it and you learn to really set some time aside that isn't work time, I mean I take my phone on holiday, I read my emails but now I don't respond to my emails on holiday, unless it's urgent, and then I delegate it to somebody else to deal with. Because otherwise, the minute you respond, people will be like, oh, she's online, she's working. I don't not read them, I'm not that good that I can ignore it completely, but I've kind of learnt to separate the two really and give the family the time they deserve and I think, with the festival being in May, we always work over Easter, over the May Bank Holiday, just straight through, but I always say to the team, take some time off, but they're like, *Oh but I've got to do this or this*, and I'm like just take a day off, go and see your family, do whatever you need to do, because nothing changes actually.

Jess: *I think it's also motivational as well because I know when I go back to work in September, I feel a little bit more excited and a little bit more hungry to get back. Although I'm really bad at turning off emails; I think I am actually addicted to email.*

Lisa: You know when something is really, really urgent, when it cannot wait, but if you look at your to-do list there is probably only one thing on there that cannot wait. I'm quite good at methodically organising my to-do list, just so, you know when you look at your list and it's 4 p.m. and you think you're not going to get it all done, I'm quite good at shifting things onto the next day's list and prioritising which three things I do actually need to get done, which can wait till the next day, and what can wait till next week. So, I think that is quite good time management really, particularly in events when you have really tight deadlines. The amount of people who just step onsite absolutely broken because they've killed themselves in the lead-up and then it's really hard. They are tough hours, and it's hard to get through it mentally, so I think you've got to put yourself in the right place and be strong enough to do the next phase, and I think the only way you can do that is give yourself some time off.

Jess: *I think that is really good advice. It feels like knowing when to have that down time and when to have that more lucid space and also being really organised and focused in your professional space and working in collaboration, and having a mentor is important for you. Is there anything else you feel your creativity needs, that you feel really boosts or helps your creativity?*

Lisa: I guess I like to look at everything else, you know, what else is going on, open your eyes, particularly on events, it's quite easy to get inside that bubble. It's really good to get some perspective and ideas and look at what other people do well. There are always things I wish we were doing. I think it's really important to just look around as well and not get too immersed in what you're doing and obviously not steal things but take influence from those things around you. Look at what did someone else did well and how you could interpret that in your own plans. But yeah, I like to be influenced by everything else that's around me constantly.

I've taken on Wilderness Festival as production director this year, which is amazing. It's probably not going to happen [due to the Covid-19 pandemic], but it's a really creative event. It's completely different to the Great Escape, and it's a real eye opener. But what I really loved about the first meeting I went to was sitting with a huge team of people and just listening to how they love it. They just ooze creativity, ideas and passion. They're talking about paddleboard yoga and things that don't enter my head. I'm not about to turn the Great Escape into Wilderness Festival, and I won't suggest we do paddleboard yoga, but looking at how different people work and how different ideas come to fruition, it gives you a bit of confidence, because you go, *Do you know what we do that much better*, or there's some things you look at and go, *That's brilliant and how can I take a bit of that into what we do?*

I worked at Pride last year as event control manager which was really interesting. It was a massive eye opener working at the heart of that event, but again there's just certain things that I took from it, *Do you know what, that is fantastic*, just little elements, *This is great, can I steal that because I really like the way you do that?* It's just taking those little bits of influence and giving you confidence in what you're doing I suppose, rather than looking at something and going, *Urgh, they're doing that much better than me*. It's just taking the positives and letting that influence you without copying it completely.

Jess: *Yeah, I think in academia there is quite a stab-in-the-back culture, and one of the people we've interviewed for the book is someone I really admire and respect because of their academic work and their writing, and she has really inspired me. And it just reminded me that it's really good to have people to look up to that remind you why you're passionate about what you do and that you can learn from as well.*

Lisa: I think for me, learning is just so important. I learn stuff every day. My work is evolving and I guess when I first started, I was promoting the shows and doing live gigs and now I've grown into event management, festival management and a lot of the stuff I do now is quite boring, licensing, health and safety, but I'm constantly learning, and it shapes the way we do things. Starting to work on other events is interesting. If I was doing the same thing every year, I think I'd be out by now to be honest. Even with the Great Escape, although the format is similar, it changes and it grows. We work with some fantastic event partners, and they bring different ideas and different venues so it never stays still, and that's really important for me. I don't think I could do it if it was the same format rolling out year on year. There's a lot of collaborators on that event and a lot of partners, and they all bring something to the table and we never quite know what shape the Great Escape is going to end up in. It evolves over the year, different people come in with different ideas, some are ridiculous, and I think we're never going to be able to do that and it shapes the event, and it keeps you learning and pushing the boundaries really.

Jess: *You've talked about developing new roles and things like the Pride and Wilderness Festival, which sound amazing, where do you hope to go next with your creativity?*

Lisa: Well, I think it's funny, I do wonder how many years I can get away with doing this job, and I do have some meetings, having very lovely lunches with thinking, *How is this a job?* It's funny with the kids because they think I'm off to work and I do have those moments when I just stop and think, *Oh I should probably get a proper job soon* and then I have days when I think, *This is a great job and I'm going to do it forever* and so I'm going to see where it takes me, I suppose. I've got no grand plan.

I think my role in events is evolving; some of the things I've been asked to come in and do, I've doubted I've been good enough to do. It's interesting how other people see you, isn't it, because I still see myself as this 20-year-old who is bumbling along doing a bit of music and it's interesting how other people view that. I'm just going to see where that takes me. I think it's really important to keep that creativity outside of work going and have a dabble with things, and I do remember sitting down with one of my colleagues onsite after a very stressful event, and we were sat in event control saying, *This is horrible, shall we just give this up?* and we decided we were going to make bunting for a living, and you know if I could just make bunting for a living it would be lovely. I wouldn't need to worry about anyone or any other people's lives, I could just make bunting and then you snap out of it the day after and go, *That'd be boring, I'll carry on and see where it takes me.* It's changing, it's interesting and I'll just see where that goes.

I've always felt really lucky. I think there's not a day goes by where I don't feel lucky to earn a living doing something I love, and my work is my friends, my passion, my life and not everyone is that fortunate. I think you create that destiny. It certainly wasn't handed to me on a plate, but there's not a day goes by when I don't appreciate that. It's interesting, the kids' perception of what I do for a living is hilarious sometimes, and they're probably my biggest critics, particularly with the design elements. They're always commenting on the designs. I'm not sure about this design this year, and they're very critical of it all, and they come to the Great Escape always on the Saturday just to have a look round. I remember having a meeting a few years ago with YouTube and when I left the house I said, *Mummy's got a meeting with YouTube today*, and he's like, what, have you actually, *yeah, yeah* and you stop and think how funny that sounds. I'll be at the school gates and I can be on the phone talking about all sorts of ridiculous things, one time I had a conversation about counterterrorism measures and evacuations and then you're at the school gates chatting, and you're thinking, *Is this really my world?* It can be quite a mad one, especially when you stop and actually think about what you actually do for a living.

Jess: *One of the things that has really come out of what you're saying is how hard you do work and the variety of things you do, but also how you have been able to maintain that passion for everything that you work on, and I think that is brilliant advice for anyone who finds themselves in a stuck place with their creativity.*

Lisa: Yeah, I think so, and I think if you are stuck like that, you've got to look around you and question why you are stuck and if you're stuck, you're probably bored or maybe it's time to stretch yourself maybe. I don't have an awful lot of time to be bored. In the downtime when things are a bit quieter, I have a few doubts or find it hard to get going again sometimes, but I never doubt what I do really, in terms of what I want to do. I've always got the strength to carry on.

Postscript

Even when the volume and magnitude of her work seems overwhelming, Lisa's experience and expertise in her field help her to believe in herself and her ability to get the job done. She has a trusted support system in place with reliable friends/mentors and family who care about and support her ambitions, also providing her with opportunities to connect with her lifelong creative practice of making, playing and finding space for rest that means she can come back feeling rejuvenated and inspired to face new challenges.

In earlier work, we looked at helping creative practice students reflect on the skills and experiences that would help them to contribute to a creative workplace (Ashmore and Moriarty, 2015). For many of us, making links between our creativity and our vocational ambitions can provide the confidence to take risks, apply for jobs and lead projects that not only enhance a community, organisation or place, but also evolve our own creative practice. Putting our creativity to work can lead to an increased sense of self-belief as practitioners, and value the contribution our work can make on the world around us. Speaking about Creative Writing, Munden (2013) argues that: "In unpredictable times, innovation will be the lifeblood of many industries: Creative Writing can produce self-motivated graduates with exceptional understandings of team process, of two-way communication and of individual creative thinking. ... They generate consumers of Literature who are of entrepreneurial spirit." (p. 36). Creative practice, not just writing, is often seen as a luxury, a frivolous and almost narcissistic act that takes place on the side, as a hobby, but of course, the world needs innovators and makers like Lisa who enrich society, making life more pleasurable and helping us escape when reality becomes bleak or too much.

Speaking to Lisa pushed me to reflect on my own working life and consider how I can encourage creativity in my students whilst making more time outside of work for my own creative space and play. Finding opportunities to rest and recover from the day, week or term gives me a renewed appetite to teach and remember what an honour it is – despite the emails!

Bibliography

Ashmore, N., & Moriarty, J. (2015). From student to artist: Supporting students' creative development through place-based work. *Journal of Writing in Creative Practice*, *8*(1), 37–54. https://doi.org/10.1386/jwcp.8.1.37_1

Munden, P. (2013). *Beyond the benchmark: Creative writing in higher education*. Higher Education Academy.

National Union of Students (2011), Race for Equality: A Report on the Experiences of Black.

Students in Further and Higher Education, London: NUS, at http://www.nus.org.uk/Page-Files/12350/NUS_Race_for_Equality_web.pdf. Accessed 8th August 2023.

CREATIVE FUTURES

A Response to Lisa Norman with Megan Bell

Jess Moriarty

Listening to Lisa, I am struck by just how successfully she has managed to make her passion her professional life. Bringing music and memories to thousands of people, uplifting audiences and providing a platform for artists to inspire and move clearly nourishes Lisa, and also enriches the lives of staff, musicians and visitors to the events she expertly manages. Whether it is the mighty Brighton Pride or the award-winning Great Escape, Lisa's events are driven by a desire to promote diversity, support live music – which is inextricably linked with enhanced well-being for all involved (Fancourt & Finn, 2019) – all while identifying materials and methods that make the gigs and festivals she manages sustainable and safe. The interview provokes me in three key ways:

1 That despite the attack on the arts (in terms of funding and post-Covid support), it is still possible to develop a career in the creative industries that is nourishing, dynamic and able to sustain a person (and their family) – this is hopeful;
2 That Lisa is a true renaissance woman – capable of maintaining her work/ personal/creative life/lives to an utterly awe-inspiring standard that I hope to learn from;
3 That she is mentored and mentors – looking up to colleagues for advice and also throwing the ladder back down to new artists and creative professionals seeking to make their own way in the industry, and this makes me reflect on my own ways of working and how I can map this onto my own practice.

DOI: 10.4324/9781003286042-15

And I am interested in what these provocations mean in terms of creativity and the future.

Pre/mid/post-Covid we need the arts to capture lived experiences, reflect them and also, help us to transcend them – this is fundamental to living well; creativity in the UK has not diminished in power, and in spite of the lack of support from our current government (Harris, 2021), Lisa has been able to prevail, just as the arts must. How then, can creativity fortify and defend itself in a time of cuts – to funding and also via the removal of creative subjects from schools (Fletcher, 2019)? Lisa's approach of developing a network that values expertise, mutual support and encouragement seems to offer a potential way of working collectively to steel ourselves and not just protect, but evolve creativity – promoting work that decolonises and celebrates diversity, is ethically minded and contributes to living well. It is an approach I have tried to factor into my own practice, and this chapter opens up a space to consider how individual and collective creativity can move into a future where the landscapes are unsure – implications for the climate, the overturning of *Roe v. Wade* in the US and data confirming that international well-being is in crisis post-Covid (Bil, Bułowa, & Świerzawski, 2021) are all indicators of a monumental global tipping point, and which way we are going to fall is not yet vivid – what is certain is that creativity and activism can play a part in the reshaping that is undoubtedly ahead.

Part of this process will inevitably involve some uncomfortable conversations about how we (creatives) ethically practice; who is and who isn't part of creative conversations and why; and how creativity can support and stimulate well-being but addressing these issues – I would argue – can offer ways of enriching and enlivening creativity too. The artist as activist is not a new concept – Haraway (2019) considers the positively blurred boundaries between the activist/scientist/artist through her own work and advocates for others to do the same – and harnessing this approach to expand and develop creativity can and will provide an essential tool, helping people to value the arts and see a place for themselves as creatives – within the cultural industries or/and in their daily lives.

In the rest of this chapter, I give examples of practice where Lisa's approach is evident, collaborating with others on projects driven by a shared social responsibility, learning from people about what I don't know and for that to be a reciprocal conversation. In this way, creative conversations are central to how creativity evolves and the interviews in this book have informed my own ways of working, forcing me to reflect and adjust. At the end of the chapter, readers will be asked to consider how the conversations in this book have impacted on their own approaches to creativity and to set intentions for what you will do next.

Uncomfortable Conversations – Rewilding Higher Education

Speaking about his life as an artist for an exhibition at the Tate Modern, William Kentridge suggests that a degree of self-reflection and an awareness of one's privilege is a wholly necessary part of the creative process. From this perspective, it is possible to contradict and critique narratives claiming certainty and construct new meanings (Kentridge, 2018). It is a position that resonates. Several years ago, I was asked to develop a chapter for an international book entitled *Surviving Sexism in Academia*, which I was delighted to be part of. I wrote about my own experiences in higher education (HE) and how as a woman, mother, writer, I had found myself often reduced and undermined. The book wanted to disrupt dominant narratives and promote change, and when I read the final publication, I was moved and inspired by what the other authors had shared and the insights they so generously offered. But my chapter fell short. Whilst it was lived and personal, it was passive. I could almost hear myself sighing in the pages and realised that my piece – the reading of it but also the process of writing it – was unexciting to me. Because I was writing autobiographically, the ideas were too known and the uncertainty and risk that is so fundamental to creative work (Beghetto, Karwowski, & Reiter-Palmon, 2021) was noticeably missing. I tell my students all the time to take chances, try new things, to dream and find out what they don't already know, but back then, I became conscious that I was failing to take the time to nourish myself and my practice in the same way.

At the same time, I heard the incredible Munroe Bergdorf – trans model, writer, presenter and activist – give an interview on Channel 4 News where she asked: "If you are saying you are not racist, then what are you doing to dismantle racism? Because you can benefit from racism and not be a racist person" (Bergdorf, 2017). And this struck a chord. Of course, I would have been horrified if anyone had accused me of racism – then or now – but as a white, middle-class, heteronormative woman, educated to the highest level in a time before universities charged students for studying, I have to acknowledge that I am hugely privileged and that I have benefited from historic racism in society and culture, including the institutionalised racism still permeating HE (Emejulu, 2017). There is no point denying or excusing this – it is real. How then to confront this privilege and produce work that might be considered part of the necessary decolonising of education and creative writing? I should say at this point that it is not my place to lecture or advise on how exactly to carry out this work – I am still working it out for myself and learning from people who rightfully own that space. Performing decolonial actions involves risks of making mistakes and reinforcing the matrix of coloniality through trying to make itself comprehensible to those disciplinary, methodological or ideological territories that hold the grip of the matrix. As Stein et al. (2020) reflect on their own work, "we can only 'gesture' toward the direction of decolonisation, and we will undoubtedly make mistakes in the process, for which we are also accountable. Yet these mistakes also offer important learning opportunities" (p. 45). Instead, I offer a window on how it has been for me in the hope that it is of interest and might prompt reflection for other creatives.

Finding out what we don't know and being prepared for inevitable mistakes can be daunting. Lisa uses mentors she respects who encourage but also speak frankly, drawing on their own expertise to guide. Similarly, the starting point in acknowledging my own uncertainty arose in a meeting with a friend and colleague, Anthony Kalume, who is the director of Diversity Lewes – a charity seeking to resist prejudice in Sussex by working with a range of community groups and services including health, schools and the police. I asked Tony his thoughts on the continuing, unresolved issues around students from the Global Ethnic Majorities (GEM).

A National Student Survey in 2011 had found that 42% of GEM students did not believe their curriculum reflected issues of diversity, equality and discrimination, and a third (34%) stated that institutions often "did not take into account diverse backgrounds and views" (NUS, 2011, p. 4). In the UK, universities are deeply gendered and racialised (Emejulu, 2017) and a later report from the NUS (NUS, 2019) identified four key areas for HE to urgently address:

1 a need for strong GEM leadership;
2 creating a culture in which it is possible to have open and honest conversations about race and racism;
3 developing racially diverse and inclusive environments and communities;
4 getting the evidence and understanding what it means and understanding what works.

But despite these recommendations, prejudice and victimisation still occur frequently amongst staff and students in HE, and most significantly affect those from marginalised groups including (but by no means only) Black, LGBTQIA+, disabled and working-class people.

A recent study found that women and Black people are still likely to suffer prejudice in UK universities (Bhopal & Henderson, 2021) and that LGBTQIA+ people are also at high risk of discrimination in education (Formby 2013; Kosciw et al., 2013, Harris et al. 2021). Students in the UK who identify as LGBTQIA+ are more likely to report lower social acceptance and student engagement (Silverschanz et al., 2008; Woodford et al., 2012) with their mental health being placed at significant risk whilst studying (Gnan et al., 2019). This all suggests that HE is still not a welcoming space to women, Black, and LGBTQIA+ students and staff, and I acknowledge that this is not the whole picture. People with disabilities and intersectional people are even more at risk, and this is further evidence of the tradition and convention that stifles HE and why "a search for a better conversation in the face of all the barriers and boundaries" (Ellis and Bochner, 2000, p. 748) is so urgently needed.

Speaking to Tony about my part in this system and my contribution to a dominant discourse that has historically excluded and undermined Black, LGBTQIA+, disabled and working-class people was awkward at first, not least because I was taking up his time and energy to educate me on a system he has been oppressed by, but Tony quickly shifted the conversation on so that it became more constructive and dynamic. In the first place he told me to stop going on about it and laughed at me, which was instantly disarming, and then suggested we develop a project to with a local museum – who were also interested in decolonisation work – and bring people together to share ideas on making historically racist spaces more inclusive. This move away from Tony mentoring me, to us sharing ideas and collaborating, meant that it became instantly more purposeful and transformative – making our shared aspirations to engage in decolonisation work active rather than passive.

We successfully applied for funding and the project went ahead (Kalume & Moriarty, 2022). Speaking with Tony, sharing ideas and being open to him challenging me is an evolution of the method that Chris and I established in earlier work (Reading & Moriarty, 2019), where we acknowledged our experiences with cancer and the effect it had had on our creativity and on us. In my work with Tony, I had to confront my privilege and the discomfort and support I found in our conversation stimulated new ways of being, thinking and practising – in my teaching and in my writing. Tony and I have published together, taught together and applied for future funding to continue this work, but this is complex, as I still benefit from all my social/professional privileges and the project needs funding to be sustainable and pay for Tony's part in it. As already mentioned, funding is harder to come by because of cuts to the arts, but the conversation we started has opened up a space that allows for meaningful and needed change – even if it is at a much slower pace than either of us would like.

This project encouraged me to look up and identify a mentor/expert (a method Lisa advocates in the interview) who could give advice on decolonising my pedagogy and practice. But when we speak of evolving HE and creativity, we must also encourage new ideas and promote new artists – something else Lisa has been able to achieve in her work. As a lecturer and editor, I am able to do this to some extent – publishing new work in the books I edit and supporting students to develop confidence with their emerging practice. The project with Tony encouraged me to consider how I might work with someone younger and less experienced than me, and I applied for funding to pay for an undergraduate student to carry out research for this book in a chapter exploring decolonising creativity. Again, I was lucky enough to be awarded funding and working on the premise that students learn best when empowered as researchers (Tinto, 2019). I devised a creative brief inviting the successful student to carry out a literature review on decolonising creativity and co-author a chapter with me – for which they would be paid as a research assistant. I thought what might emerge was that the student/research assistant would benefit from the experience and that the chapter would be better for the new perspective, but again, what the conversations with Megan (co-author) actually engendered was something new, surprising, dynamic. It moved me away from the concept of myself as an academic expert – a problematic notion that is synonymous with traditional academic work (Moriarty, 2019) – and rebalanced the power dynamic between us, helping me to see Megan as a collaborator rather than a mentee. For me, mentorship and being mentored is best experienced as a conversation where power is shared. Conversations have been critiqued as inferior to mentorship because they lack purpose (Mullen & Klimatis, 2021), but the model Chris and I have developed forefronts intention setting and shared purpose from the outset as a way of stimulating creativity and producing creative outputs (Reading & Moriarty, 2022). Working in this way, conversation can lead to new ideas and new work (creative/critical) and be part of the decolonial turn, bringing people into research instead of excluding and privileging only a few. In this chapter, whilst I have written the text, it is Megan who carried out the research and whose advice and feedback shaped and informed my writing. Therefore, I see this as our chapter despite the first person narrator.

In our first meeting, Megan was quick to point out that two white women writing a chapter on decolonising creativity was problematic – the performative gesture – and suggested instead that we focus on approaches and methods that might help readers to reflect on their existing creative practices and their own activism – public or personal. We talked about how our creativity had helped us to navigate sexism and misogyny and identified poetry as a medium we both use to think through lived experiences with patriarchy, seeing our writing as a form of resistance (Moriarty, 2019).

As writers, we saw our collaboration as an opportunity to produce creative work in the spirit of social justice, offering a resistance to dominant oppressive structures, often synonymous with traditional academic work (Moriarty, 2019). As Hunt argues, by fictionalising our own autobiography, the writer is able to move beyond entrapment in a single image of herself and to expand the possibilities for self (Hunt, 2000), and working in this way, Megan and I are able to express our lived/imaginary experiences and feel differently about those experiences.

In the poem below, I invoke the goddess Persephone, who was forced to live in the underworld by her husband, Hades. Greek myths are dominated by male heroes and male perspectives and recently, rewriting women in these stories has become a way of giving voice to the voiceless (Barker, 2019; Miller, 2019). My Persephone is also me, but by bleeding our stories together, I have created a fiction that helps me to see myself as not trapped and overwhelmed by the domestic/professional juggle, but creative, expansive – in control of my imaginatively written ending, but also my own life. This method is creative and imaginative but also my own activism, invoking a goddess to help me to feel differently about my lived experiences and move on from them. In my story, Hades' gender is not defined, and I imagine them as non-binary. This allows me to feel differently about their agency – in this story, Persephone is not controlled by a man; instead, she is given space to liberate herself by a non-binary partner.

Persephone

How can I please you mother,
Teacher, brother, peer reviewer, boyfriend,
Partner, husband, lover, friend from school, friend from gym,
Nurse at smear test, next of kin,
Midwife, surgeon, breast feeding trainer,
Waxer, taxer, therapist, student, colleague, nemesis,
Bank manager, life insurer, younger sis.
Builder, baker, my own maker, newborn, new one, stepson,
Nan?
How can I bring your spring, your summer,
Urge you from the winter mother,
How can I always be your sunrise when
The night in me wants her say?

How can I please you with my 6 weeks too early, too late to have a baby,
Too tall in the school photo, too nice to get promoted, too sarcastic in meetings,
Too much, too too much,
Too many crisps, too many cigarettes, too many drinks, too many pills –
green and yellow, smiley faces and
Red like pomegranate seeds.
Too much homework, too many friends, too often on the phone,
Too fucking smart, too gay, definitely too fat to get fucked.
Too much staying in then too much going out,
Too many clothes, too much flesh, too obvious, too little,
Too many boys, too much choice, too much no choice at all.
Too feminist, too much asking for it, too high, too hard when I fell.

All these wanting faces, wanting me to be more, do more, give more.
Never quite enough.
When Hades came, they did not drag me off the way father had it said,
My story and my mother's – always his, never ours,
Him the hero and us bit parts in his one-sided play.
When Hades came,
I was tired. In the garden planting seeds to please my mother,

They offered me their hand, their kingdom and said:
Please yourself.
Myself?
And I dared wonder how that might look and feel and smell and sound and taste
And I wanted to try it on, twirl around and say:
It fits just right.

In the Underworld, at first, I did not know
What I then was,
My hands and legs would flit and flinch,
A Frankenstein of what I might be.
A queen, I thought, should help
The souls who seek the sun but no,
Their journeys are their own and then
I tried to make my marriage work
But Hades only laughed when I did the
Things I'd learnt to keep the peace.
Please yourself.
They said again and I
Gave in.

And now I know myself, my joy
Is to live life for me and not a
Boy or Zeus who would not share
The light and made my mother
Frozen, white. Now when I return
To her embrace, her warmth and love
Her tender face, she knows that while it
Brings her woe, back to my queendom I will go.
In summer, I am at her side
But in my realm, I now reside
My new found bliss? Not on my knees
But on my feet with me to please.
Not too much but just enough,
A woman I have come to love.
        (Moriarty, 2021 in Marr & Moriarty, 2021)

Define 'Feminine'

Megan Bell
Divine feminine is
Displayed when I'm on my knees,

Waiting upon your hour of need,
Gazing up through my lashes,
The 'feminine' displayed:
I make my face wide,
Slightly afraid
At the way my body folds
And morphs at your touch,
Which doesn't take much.
Does my absent stare make you hard
When I catch your glare and hold it?

An actor on your personal stage,
Bottled rage that lasts an age,
The whispers of protest sing in my ear
From ancestral sisters,
As the man says down …
and I kneel.
This is an escape from the anger I feel
In the light of day.
I admit it's not very *feminist* of me.

On the contrary,

I am a walking, erotic desire.
Tall and blonde and powerful in
White leather boots
Men beg to be stepped on.
They fall out of their stained vans,
Gluttonous bellies scraping the pavement
As they crawl towards my feet.
And that's the puzzle.
Which one is me? Really?
Define 'feminine'.

Conclusion – Where We Want Creativity to Go

Lisa's interview inspired reflection on my own practice and how I have used creative conversations to inform and evolve my own creative practice to resist and challenge dominant narratives and work ethically with collaborators to share power and produce new work. This approach has encouraged me to decolonise my methods of working and think of myself as artist/activist, and this makes me feel positive about how I might use my creativity going forward to be part of societal change. My conversations with Megan and Tony had shared utopian goals that include:

- mutual trust;
- valuing of each partner's expertise and experience;
- shared purpose concerned with decolonising creativity and academic work;
- recognition of the artist as activist;
- shared power – although this is still complex and ongoing.

But this is far from definitive or perfect, and that is okay. Being open to learning from others, being wrong and a willingness to change can enliven our creative work and offer an important tool in how creativity can and will contribute to conversations around diversity, climate change and living well (Fancourt & Finn, 2019). In this sense we can all be open to evolving and for that to be supported by our creativity and creative community.

Creative Task

Think about your response to the chapters and conversations in this book. How have they and/or how might they change your own creative process and practice? Do you think of yourself as an activist and if not, what cause does your – or could your – work respond to in a spirit of social justice and positive change? What conversations do you need to have to support you with this?

Bibliography

Barker, P. (2019). *The silence of the girls*. Penguin.

Beghetto, R. A., Karwowski, M., & Reiter-Palmon, R. (2021). Intellectual risk taking: A moderating link between creative confidence and creative behavior? *Psychology of Aesthetics, Creativity, and the Arts, 15*(4), 637.

Bergdorf, M. (2017). Transgender model speaks on racism. *Channel 4 News*, 2 September 2017. https://www.facebook.com/Channel4News/videos/101551 99708451939/ Accessed 6 January 2023.

Bhopal, K., & Henderson, H. (2021). Competing inequalities: Gender versus race in higher education institutions in the UK. *Educational Review, 73*(2), 153–169.

Bil, J. S., Buława, B., & Świerzawski, J. (2021). Mental health and the city in the post-COVID-19 era. *Sustainability, 13*(14), 7533.

Ellis, C. S., & Bochner, A. (2000). Autoethnography, personal narrative, reflexivity: Researcher as subject. In N. K. Denzin, & Y. S. Lincoln (Eds.), *Collecting and interpreting qualitative materials* (2nd ed., pp. 733–768). Sage Publications.

Emejulu, A. (2017). Feminism for the 99%: Towards a populist feminism? *Soundings, 66*(Summer). Retrieved May 10 2018, from https://www.lwbooks.co.uk/soundings/66/towards-populist-feminism

Fancourt, D., & Finn, S. (2019). *What is the evidence on the role of the arts in improving health and well-being? A scoping review.* World Health Organization. Regional Office for Europe.

Fletcher, R. (2019). Public libraries, arts and cultural policy in the UK. *Library Management.*

Formby, E. (2013). Understanding and responding to homophobia and bullying: Contrasting staff and young people's views within community settings in England. *Sexuality Research and Social Policy, 10*(4), 302–316.

Gnan, G. H., Rahman, Q., Ussher, G., Baker, D., West, E., & Rimes, K. A. (2019). General and LGBTQ-specific factors associated with mental health and suicide risk among LGBTQ students. *Journal of Youth Studies, 22*(10), 1393–1408.

Haraway, D. (2019). It matters what stories tell stories; it matters whose stories tell stories. *A/b: Auto/Biography Studies, 34*(3), 565–575.

Harris, G. (2021). UK government approves 50% funding cut for arts and design courses (theartnewspaper.com). Accessed 4 January 2023.

Harris, R., Wilson-Daily, A. E., & Fuller, G. (2021). Exploring the secondary school experience of LGBT+ youth: An examination of school culture and school climate as understood by teachers and experienced by LGBT+ students. *Intercultural Education, 32*(4), 368–385.

Hunt, C. (2000). *Therapeutic dimensions of autobiography in creative writing.* Jessica Kingsley Publishers.

Kalume, T., & Moriarty, J. (2022). "It's a collaborative affair": Case studies of innovative practice in and across HE. In *The Bloomsbury handbook of collaboration in higher education: Tales from the frontline.* Bloomsbury. Accepted/In press.

Kentridge, W. (2018). William Kentridge: 'Art must defend the uncertain' | *Tate.* https://www.tate.org.uk/art/artists/william-kentridge-2680/william-kentridge-art-must-defend-uncertain. Accessed 5 January 2023.

Kosciw, J. G., Palmer, N. A., Kull, R. M., et al. (2013). The effect of negative school climate on academic outcomes for LGBT youth and the role of inschool supports. *Journal of School Violence, 12*(1), 45–63.

Marr, V., & Moriarty, J. (2021). Reclaiming stories: Invoking the goddess. *Gramarye Journal,* (20). http://www.sussexfolktalecentre.org/journal/

Miller, M. (2019). *Circe.* Bloomsbury Publishing.

Moriarty, J. (2019). *Autoethnographies from the neoliberal academy: Rewilding, writing and resistance in higher education.* (1st ed.) Routledge.

Mullen, C. A., & Klimatis, C. C. (2021). Defining mentoring: A literature review of issues, types, and applications. *Annals of the New York Academy of Sciences, 1483*(1), 19–35.

National Union of Students and Universities UK, Black, Asian and Minority Ethnic Student Attainment at UK Universities: #Closingthegap 2019 https://www.universitiesuk.ac.uk/policy-and-analysis/reports/Documents/2019/bame-student-attainment-uk-universities-closingthe-gap.pdf. Accessed 4 October 2019.

National Union of Students and Universities UK, Race for Equality: A report on the experiences of Black students in further and higher education: https://www.nus.org.uk/PageFiles/12350/NUS_Race_for_Equality_web.pdf Downloaded 15 October 2019.

Reading, C., & Moriarty, J. (2019). Walking and mapping our creative recovery: An interdisciplinary method. In J. Moriarty (Ed.), *Autoethnographies from the neoliberal academy: Rewilding, writing and resistance.* Routledge.

Reading, C., & Moriarty, J. (2022). *Walking for creative recovery: A handbook for creatives with insights and ideas for supporting your creative life*. Triarchy Press.

Silverschanz, P., Cortina, L. M., Konik, J., & Magley, V. J. (2008). Slurs, snubs, and queer jokes: Incidence and impact of heterosexist harassment in academia. *Sex Roles, 58*(3), 179–191.

Stein, S., Andreotti, V., Suša, R., Amsler, S., Hunt, D., Ahenakew, C., & Okano, H. (2020). Gesturing towards decolonial futures: Reflections on our learnings thus far. *Nordic Journal of Comparative and International Education, 4*(1).

Tinto, V. (2019). Learning better together. In *Transitioning students into higher education* (pp. 13–24). Routledge.

Woodford, M. R., Silverschanz, P., Swank, E., Scherrer, K. S., & Raiz, L. (2012). Predictors of heterosexual college students' attitudes toward LGBT people. *Journal of LGBT Youth, 9*(4), 297–320.

CONCLUSION

Centring Your Creative Life

Christina Reading and Jess Moriarty

Creativity and the arts have always held up a mirror to what is happening in the world, to remind us of the extraordinary beauty, but to also problematise the world we have created and must take responsibility for. How we respond to the climate emergency, global well-being crisis, and strive to include and value all people instead of privileging just a few still motivates the work of contemporary artists. From the ultimate renaissance man, Stormzy, encouraging us to "f**k Boris" (2019) whilst simultaneously raising awareness about knife violence at Glastonbury, to Tan Zi Xi's installation that uses plastic waste (Plastic Ocean, 2016) found in the oceans to confront our reliance on materials that are choking the planet and via the insights into mental health using poetry and image that kept Rupi Kaur's *Milk and Honey* (2015) in the *New York Times* bestseller list for over a year, contemporary artists have used their work to stimulate debate and highlight issues in the spirit of social justice and a desire for meaningful change. These examples are prolific, important but the conversations in this book have helped us – Chris and Jess – to acknowledge that creativity can and will bring meaningful change, and that can be personal, professional, profound. Perhaps now more than ever, the social responsibility of not just the artist, but of all of us, is undeniable. The planet is on a tipping point that feels overwhelming, and the future potentially unchangeable from the apocalyptic trajectory we seem to be on. In these moments of uncertainty and fear, our creative endeavours might feel futile, but we argue that Creative Conversations offer a way of connecting, reimagining, motivating with even a promise of hope.

Can a conversation change or save the world? In isolation, perhaps this is idealistic and naïve, but in our earlier work, we found that our method of talking about our creativity – concerns and challenges, ambitions and

DOI: 10.4324/9781003286042-16

dreams – helped to entice us out of the hibernation that cancer had frozen us in. In this book, opening these conversations up beyond our own experience to the brilliant women we spoke to has fortified our belief in the power of conversation to motivate our creativity and also, to support us – all of us – to live well.

Speaking with Thomasina, Anna, Griz, Irene, Katarina, Lisa and Sonia exceeded our initial expectations – their words are expert, intelligent, personal and motivating. Each of them has identified strategies that have enabled them to excel in their creative lives, developing ways of being that centre their creativity as fundamental to who they are – professionally and personally. It is almost impossible to sum up their rich and generous insights – each time we have reread the conversations, we take something new and nourishing that encourages reflection on our own creativity and a way of deepening our understanding of ourselves.

Each reader will take something bespoke from the book, and it is our hope that reading the conversations and engaging with the creative tasks will have fortified or reignited your own creativity. Now that the book has ended, why not set an intention for a new creative project that can maintain the momentum you have started here? Something that reflects a creative epiphany that the book may have triggered or reawakened that you identify as being purposeful and part of meaningful change. For us, those epiphanies have included but are not restricted to:

Creativity is a process of looking back and reaching forward – value the archive of lived experiences and knowledge your body already holds and use that to motivate new projects;

Creativity needs new ideas – develop new connections, carry out research, inhabit unfamiliar spaces that will push your creativity in new directions;

Creativity can create change – whether this is a quiet, loud or personal type of activism, allow your creativity to have a social purpose that you value as part of living well;

Creativity matters – that despite the attack on funding and creative subjects in schools, it is still possible to have a creative life that will sustain you;

Creativity needs uncomfortable conversations – around privilege and diversity and we – Chris and Jess included – must all work to problematise and evolve creative practice that fails to democratise creativity;

Creativity needs connection – conversations with existing members of your creative community and also new members of that community will nourish and inspire your creative work, helping you to value yourself and your practice.

Thanks doesn't quite go far enough in terms of expressing our gratitude to the incredible women who shared their stories with us. We hope that their uplifting and wise words will help readers to value their own creative endeavours, evolve and inspire their unique processes, and celebrate their individual and connected creative lives. For us, this has not only enhanced and revived our creativity via our work for this book, but also amplified our sense of our how our creativity can contribute to meaningful social change.

Creative Task

The conversations in this book have inspired Jess and Chris to think about how their next project will combine creativity and activism to respond to the well-being and eco-crises and push them to address issues of diversity and inclusion in their creative research. What will you do next? Set your intention for a new project that values your existing skills and expertise, but that also opens up new conversations that will inspire new ways of being in your creative life.

Bibliography

Kaur, R. (2015). *Milk and honey*. Andrews McMeel Publishing.
Stormzy. (2019). Videos - Stormzy - Glastonbury 2019 - BBC Accessed 26 January 2023.
Zi Xi, T. (2016). Interview with Tan Zi Xi for Oceanic Global, Tan Zi Xi – Oceanic Global. Accessed 26 January 2023.

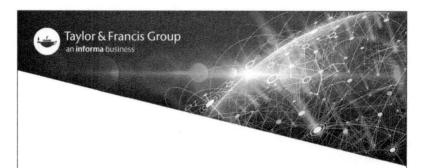